JOHN BLY, F.R.S.A.

Discovering
English Furniture

SHIRE PUBLICATIONS LTD

ACKNOWLEDGEMENTS

Cover design by Ron Shaddock. Figs 1 to 65 and 84 to 88 drawn by Robin Ollington. Figs 66 to 83 are taken from *Modern Furniture – Original and Select* by J. Lovegrove Holt, published by Jenks and Holt, wholesale and export cabinet manufacturers, upholsterers and looking-glass factors.

ISBN 0 85263 359 9. No. 223 in the 'Discovering' series.

'Discovering English Furniture 1500-1720' and 'Discovering English Furniture 1720-1830' first published 1971. 'Discovering Victorian and Edwardian Furniture' first published 1973. This combined and revised edition, with twenty-five additional photographs, first published 1976.

CONTENTS

INTRODUCTION

The story of old English furniture has in the past been divided into four main periods up to the beginning of the nineteenth century—those of Oak, Walnut, Mahogany and Satinwood. Furniture made between 1800 and 1830 is generally known as Regency, although the political Regency lasted only from 1811 to 1820. The term Regency drifts somewhat obscurely into William IV and Victorian, for it is only during the last fifteen years that any serious study has been made of this interim period, and still more recently of the Victorian itself.

The subject is both simple and complex. Simple because the stages of acquiring a basic knowledge follow a pattern related to the development of the industry itself, and complex because the periods of change or transition are directly linked with the economic, political, international and social development of our history. While it is true that all domestic articles reflect to some degree the disposition of people at any given time, furniture is the one commodity to be found in every household since our earliest civilisations. Therefore a study of English furniture is made much easier if accompanied by an understanding of the life and times of the period in question. The history of English furniture is a development: one method of construction led to another; one design formed the basis for another or created a demand for change. Either the natural invention of the craftsman or influence from abroad and the other factors mentioned above were responsible for these changes.

So it is impossible to understand fully any one period of English furniture without first knowing something of its background. A study of Victorian furniture encompasses Elizabethan, Gothic, Rustic, and New Sheraton designs as well as the French, Italian, and other 'typical' Victorian styles. These cannot truly be recognised unless something is known of the original, which in turn evolved from an earlier style or was caused by a specific reason and made in a way peculiar to that time, taking into consideration the materials available or in vogue and the tools at hand. The basic ground knowledge is simple, the pattern can be learnt. But once over the threshold, complexity begins, and the study of just one designer or maker, of one type of article or of one period can easily become a lifetime's interest. The study of English furniture is always stimulating. It can also be completely absorbing for one reason—no one person has ever, and will ever, know it all.

THE SIXTEENTH CENTURY

Tudor 1500-1558

The population in England in 1500 was just under five million —less than the number of people living in the Greater London area today and approximately one-tenth of our present population. We were over halfway through the reign of Henry VII (1485-1509), the first of the Tudors, and had yet to experience the rule of Henry VIII (1509-1547) and the monumental breakaway from the Church of Rome. The Reformation was a regrettable period when churches throughout the land were desecrated and the fittings, windows, memorials, floors and wall paintings were destroyed. So too were many of the early Nottingham alabaster figures and thousands of ounces of fine silverware. For many centuries we had had an extremely high standard of craftsmanship in building and decorating, but this had for the main part been applied to the Church. Under the feudal system, which existed until the late fifteenth and early sixteenth centuries, personal fortunes were quickly gained and lost. Much depended on physical strength and the ability to rouse some local inhabitants to take up arms against an unfriendly neighbour, and the larger houses were built as strongly fortified as possible.

Therefore, the pre-Elizabethan furniture in this country was sparse and basically utilitarian. The bed, the most important household article at this time, the chest, the table and benches had to be moved sometimes in haste because of an all too frequent house fire or a sudden attack. Wealth was displayed by the fineness of the banners and other wall hangings, the amount of silverware and gold on display, and the quality of the blankets on the bed. All of these could be packed quickly into the chest and carried to safety, the rest of the furniture being made either collapsible and portable, or expendable.

What decoration there was on domestic furniture had for centuries taken its theme from ecclesiastic style and design like the arch shapes of doors and windows. This was done by carving in low relief, fig. 1, chip carving, or by decorating with bright paint. A fine example of chip carving, i.e. cutting away the surface of the wood in small regular chunks so as to form the pattern, can be seen in plate 2. The more common use of this type of carving was on the outer edges of the early chests, the main parts being left plain. Examples of this type of chest can still be found today, but fine ones are rare. The paint used on furniture followed the application of a grain filler, see Gesso page 25, and was a kind of tempera.

The Church style decoration continued—certainly in rural

Fig. 1: A five board chest, showing low relief carving in the Gothic style popular until the period of the Reformation, and sometimes used in conjunction with the medallion heads or arcaded fronts of the Renaissance styles thereafter until the latter part of the sixteenth century.

Fig. 2: A five board chest showing the medallion head carved decoration popular during the early Renaissance in England, the first half of the sixteenth century.

England—well into the sixteenth century, and is described as Gothic. By the early sixteenth century, however, another pattern had become popular. This was the carving of chest fronts with medallion heads, fig. 2.

Religious persecution and general unrest continued under the Council of Regency of the young Edward VI (1547-1553) who was only sixteen when he died, and the short reign of Queen Mary (1553-1558). But by now feudalism was dead and instead of fighting amongst themselves the warring barons joined in the seemingly endless campaigns on the Continent. Here it was found that the French, during their invasions into Italy, had noted that the Italians were reappraising their earlier art forms, and subsequently had introduced to the courts of France a contemporary Italian style. As this was a revival of previous designs, the French called it the Renaissance.

Naturally, new ideas of design filtered back to England, and because ecclesiastical design was at a standstill, our craftsmen turned their skills to domestic work. During the latter part of the sixteenth century they were encouraged by a more peaceful England and a home life more as we know it today. One example of direct Italian Renaissance influence was the shape of the Savonarola folding chair, fig. 3. The original was designed and made for Girolamo Savonarola, a Dominican friar introduced to Florence by Lorenzo Medici and who, ironically, was to preach strongly against the Medici family and the Renaissance while still under Lorenzo's patronage. English chairs of the sixteenth century in the shape of the savonarola are extremely rare, but the chair was much copied during the latter part of the nineteenth century.

Until the seventeenth century most English furniture was

made of oak, the rest being cottage furniture of the more remote parts of the country where ash, elm, beech or anything else that was readily available might have been used. Unfortunately, being less durable than oak, hardly any early English fruitwood furniture has survived. The oak used was not English oak,

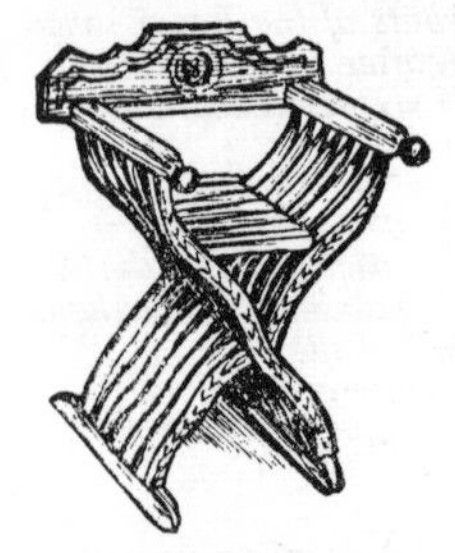

Fig. 3: A 'Savonarola' folding chair. Similar chairs are referred to in English manuscripts of the sixteenth century, following the appearance of the 'Savonarola' in Italy during the time of the Renaissance. Original examples are extremely rare, but the design was much copied during the Victorian period.

Fig. 4: A five board seat typical of the early sixteenth century. Clearly shown are the heads of either wooden pegs or hand-made iron nails securing the joints.

however. This, with its natural stout curving branches and short trunk, was thought suitable only for building ships and houses. Instead we imported oak from Norway and the Baltic countries. Furniture construction was a basic plank or slab method, the five board seat being a typical example, fig. 4. Two equal pieces of wood formed each end, two more formed the front and back, and a fifth made the seat or top. The two ends were often cut with a large inverted V to make four simple feet and the joints were secured with large hand-made nails or pegs. The dining table was merely two or three long planks joined to form a top, resting on two or three trestles. In winter the fire was built in the centre of the main hall, the smoke drifting up to the large barnlike roof to escape where it could, and the dining table was placed along the side of the hall. The master and lady of the house sat at the centre of the table with their guests and members of the household on their right and left respectively, all facing the fire. With the exception of the hosts, who had simple box-like seats with high backs and solid arms, everyone sat on stools or benches, using the wall for support.

The chest, second to the bed in importance, was used in many ways. It could stand in the dining room for use as an additional seat, and there are records of some with the tops inset with contrasting coloured woods to make chessboards. Invariably there was a chest at the foot of the bed to hold linen or, as one early manuscript suggests, the occasional lover.

The bed itself was the most sophisticated piece of furniture in the house. The four rails which formed the frame were bored with regularly spaced holes. Ropes were then threaded through and stretched across from side to side and from head to foot, thus making a pliant and strong base for the mattress. This was filled with rushes and wool or, in the better houses, feathers and down. Over the mattress went the finest wool sheets and blankets.

During the fifteenth century a method of setting a thin plank of wood within a framework of thicker pieces had been devised. The joints of the frame were made with a tongue on one piece fitting into a precut slot in the other, known as a mortice and tenon joint (mortesse and tennant *sic*). The joints were dry —without glue—and allowed sufficient movement for the wood to expand and contract without cracking, but were tight enough to stop the whole thing falling apart. The next step was to peg these joints. Before final construction one or two holes were bored in the mortice and tenon parts slightly off centre from

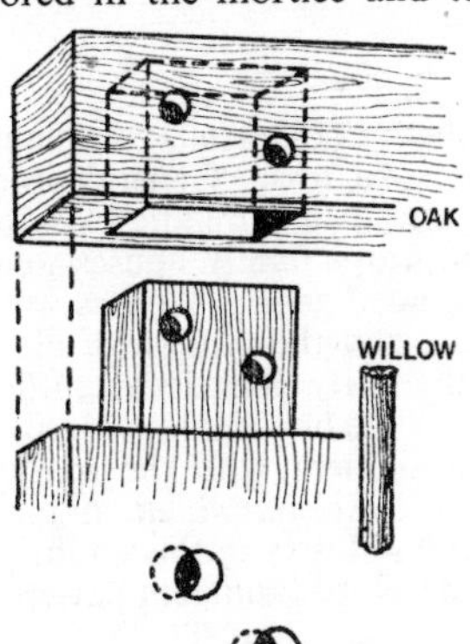

Fig. 5: The construction of a mortice and tenon joint. Originally called a 'mortesse and tennant' the latter part fitted into a precut slot in which one or two holes had been bored. The tenon was marked, removed, and then bored with two holes off centre from those in the mortice. When placed together again split willow pegs were driven in to secure the joint.

each other so that when joined in place an incomplete circle could be seen when looking through the joint, fig. 5. Into these holes willow pegs were driven, thus drawing the two parts tightly together. Willow was used because it has a long fibrous grain, and when split (not cut) into pegs and driven into position in a pegged joint it is almost impossible to break. The use of panelling and joining in the construction of furniture continued well into the seventeenth century, and the man responsible for the frame making was known as a 'joyner'. Hence our early 'joyned' or joint stools, fig. 6. A guide, but not a rule, to the authenticity of an early piece of furniture made in this way is the fact that the ends of the pegs which were driven in from the outside, were rarely cut off inside, and protrude anything up to half an inch inside the frame. This applies to the underside of seat rails and other places where, with normal use, they would not be seen or cause an obstruction.

Fig. 6: A 'joyned' or joint stool of the type dating from the early 1600s. The pegged joints are clearly visible, as are the ends of the pegs on the top. All external peg ends may protrude fractionally, see 'Wood Behaviour' page 185. Joint stools were most popular during the seventeenth century.

Elizabethan, 1558-1603

With the accession of Queen Elizabeth I (1558-1603), England faced a period of internal peace and progress. General prosperity spread through the country, and a new middle class of tradesmen and businessmen emerged. Large family houses were no longer peculiar to the titled and landed gentry. Houses were built for stable and secure family life, and the pattern of class distinction as it was known until the early twentieth century was set. Servants and other members of the household no longer took food, wine, and enjoyed entertainment with the master and his family. They had their own quarters, which in time became very important to the furniture industry in this country. And so with different patterns of life developed different patterns of furniture.

The dining hall became much more as we would recognise it today. The fire was built into the wall and the dining table placed in the middle of the room. Although still the same long rectangular shape, the supports were now four or six bulbous, turned legs, fig. 7, built into a frame with horizontal members, called

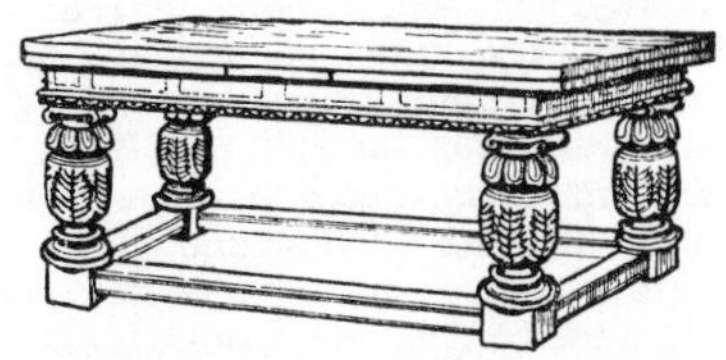

Fig. 7: An Elizabethan extending dining table on 'double cup' or 'cup and cover' turned and carved supports. This shape is repeated on contemporary bed posts and on the front supports on buffets and court cupboards. The two ends of the lower top each have two long runners fixed to the underside; when pulled out the weight of the full length top rests on these runners and supports the two leaves. This type of dining table was popular throughout the seventeenth century, the turned legs becoming progressively more slender.

stretchers, six to eight inches from the floor and the same at the top forming a frieze rail or apron. On finer furniture the rails were often decorated with carving or simple types of inlay. The stools and benches were often made and decorated to match the table and were placed all round it. To compensate for the lack of a wall to lean against a back was built on to each stool and thus the dining chair became established as an article of domestic furniture.

As furniture became more ornate and diverse in use, more skill was needed in its manufacture. Considering the tools available, joiners were capable of high degrees of accuracy in

Fig. 8: A country turner's pole lathe. A young springy tree was either used where it grew or was cut and set at an angle to be worked through a hole in the roof of the turner's shed. Turning by this method continued in some rural areas throughout the nineteenth century.

joining, pegging, carving and turning. This applied more to the country craftsmen, for in London and other major cities joining, turning and carving were mostly separate occupations. In rural areas turning was done with a pole lathe, fig. 8. A young springy tree was cut and set at an angle with a rope attached to its tip. The end of the rope was joined to a thinner cord. The piece of timber to be turned was mounted in a simple lathe, the cord wound around it and the end attached to a treadle on the floor. The spring in the tree pulled the rope up, and pressure on the treadle pulled it down, causing the piece of wood to spin first one way and then the other. Turning by this method continued in some parts of England until well into the nineteenth century, and the majority of pre-1800 fruitwood, yew and beech turned parts, such as legs, stretchers, spindles for chair backs and cupboard door panels, fig. 9, were made in this way.

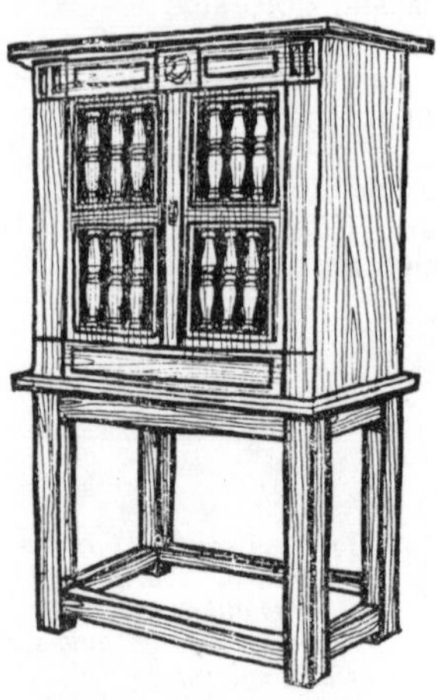

Fig. 9: A food cupboard with panels of turned spindles forming grill doors. Dating from the late sixteenth/early seventeenth centuries, this type of cupboard was made, certainly in rural areas, for the next two hundred years with slight modifications according to contemporary decoration.

By the end of the sixteenth century our houses were becoming quite full of hitherto little known articles of furniture. Food cupboards with doors that swung open on two iron pin pivots became popular, many with panels of turned spindles forming a grill, fig. 9. These were usually at eye level and supported on another cupboard base or on four turned legs with a drawer in the frieze. There were endless variations on this idea of a cupboard on a stand, the two most popular being the buffet or court cupboard and the hall cupboard, fig. 10. A feature common to nearly all this type of cupboard furniture is that the top part was set back a little to form a narrow shelf, while the top rail protrudes in line with the base to form a canopy. In early pieces this was supported by a bulbous turned column at each front corner, probably matching the turned legs of the dining table, stools and chairs. During the seventeenth century these columns tended to be cut off, leaving a canopy with a large turned pendant drop at each front corner. The earlier design was often made to match the bed posts. Elizabethan beds were highly decorated with carving, having two turned posts at the foot supporting a canopy extending from the high, panelled head board. This was hung with fine cloth drapes and tapestry curtains, fig. 11. So by the turn of the sixteenth century we had reached the age of the well appointed household and were about to embark on one of the most important and exciting periods in the history of furniture.

Fig. 10: An oak hall cupboard showing the turned pendants below the canopy. The more usual form on seventeenth century examples is the use of full turned columns in this position. Their function can be attributed to the earlier court and hall cupboards wherein the two end panels of the top half receded at an angle from the front centre section forming a splay front effect; the columns thus supporting the canopy as well as being decorative. The shaped panels of the lower half of this cupboard are peculiar to the middle and late eighteenth century as are the 'swan-neck' handles. Most oak cupboard furniture made during the seventeenth and eighteenth centuries can be dated in this way.

Fig. 11: An Elizabethan bed showing the bulbous turned front supports similar to those on tables and cupboards of the period. It continued with these proportions from 1600 until the early eighteenth century.

THE SEVENTEENTH CENTURY

Jacobean, 1603-1625

The accession of James I of England, James VI of Scotland, began what we know as the Jacobean period. James I was the first king of a legally united kingdom but, unlike many of his successors, he had little personal effect on the styles of furniture and design generally. He was overfond of hunting and drinking, preoccupied with religious discontent and not concerned with tastes and fashions. He therefore contributed little to the development of furniture. It was mainly influence from the Continent, coupled with the inventiveness of our own craftsmen that supplied new and more advanced methods of meeting the needs of society. Furniture became more ornate, with frequent use of deeper carving. One significant change in a particular motif was the gradual elongation of the bulbous 'double cup' or 'cup and cover', turning it into a more vase-like shape, see fig. 12, C and D. Concurrent with this change was another new and popular motif known today as 'bobbin turning', see fig. 12, A and B. This gives the appearance of a number of balls joined together in a straight line, sometimes interspersed with rings. It demanded a careful choice of timber, for although first used for legs and rails only, complete chairs were soon made with every member turned in this pattern and long grained wood was needed for strength. It was found also that pieces of bobbin-turned wood could be cut in half and then applied to the carcase —the basic framework of chest furniture—as well as to drawer fronts and cupboard doors.

From the simple drawer sliding in and out on the carcase frame and the drawer bottom were developed the highly efficient side 'runners'. During the early seventeenth century the utility value of a piece of furniture with several sliding drawers became apparent, but when the drawers were full their weight caused them to rub on the supporting rail in the carcase. So the drawer bottom was made to extend beyond the width of the drawer, the resultant two 'lips' running in slots cut into the carcase. To hide the slots when the drawer was in place the drawer front was made larger than the opening in the carcase. Soon, however, two proper drawer runners were added. Each of these was a strip of hard wood, approximately $\frac{3}{4}$in. x $\frac{1}{2}$in., placed in the carcase midway between the top and bottom of the drawer opening at each side and running from front to back. A groove, called a rabbet, was then worked into the sides of the drawer to accommodate the runner and the problem was solved, see plate 3. Previously seldom used in anything other than the base parts of buffets, a single long drawer, or two short

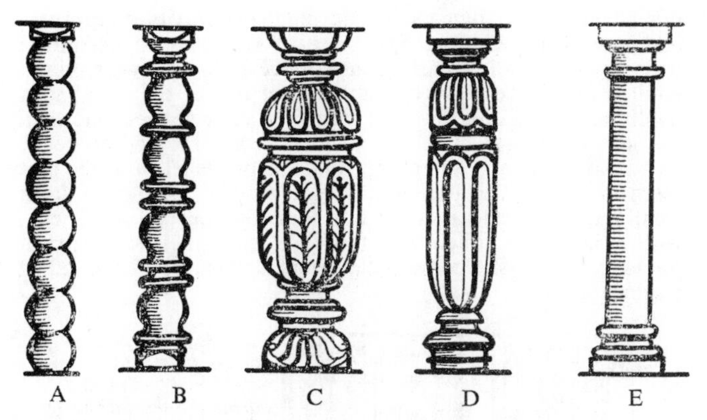

Fig. 12: Five types of turned and carved supports used on chairs, stools and tables during the seventeenth century. The following approximate dates are when these designs were most popular. (a) Knob or bobbin turning, 1630-1675. (b) Ball and ring or bobbin turning, 1640-1675. (c) Double cup or cup and cover, often carved with fluting, 1580-1690. (d) Fluted baluster, 1600-1700. (e) Pillar, 1605-1675.

drawers side by side were now being built into the bases of chest furniture. Consisting of part chest and part drawers, such pieces became very popular and because of the hybrid construction became known as 'mule' chests. Extremely fine examples can be found dating from the mid eighteenth century but popularity for them declined after 1820.

The use of sliding parts in furniture also gave us the extending or draw leaf dining table. First introduced during the late sixteenth century, this type of table became popular in the Jacobean period. Variations of the draw leaf construction were produced throughout the ensuing periods to the present day, and many of our modern extending tables work on the same basic principle as the Elizabethan version, see fig. 7. When closed the table looks like a refectory or long dining table with a double top on a rectangular frame supported by four turned legs. The top lifts up and from each end a leaf of timber the same width and almost half the length of the top is pulled out. Each of these leaves has attached to the underside two 'lopers' or extended runners the same length as the table. When both leaves are pulled out the centre part drops down level with the two leaves and its weight pressing on the four lopers supports the two ends.

By the beginning of the Jacobean period a crude form of inlay, of which there are some records during the late sixteenth century, had gained recognition. The piece of wood to be decorated had drawn on to it a pattern, usually of stylised flowers, vines, tendrils and leaves, which was then cut out of the wood to a depth of up to a quarter of an inch. The same shapes were then formed with other materials such as ivory, mother of pearl, woods of holly, box and ebony, and the pieces let in to the first piece of wood. The use of this type of inlay developed from small panels to general decoration for rails, friezes, frames, etc., with either the scrolled vine motif or with small symmetrical pieces of wood in alternating colours applied in bands called chequer inlay.

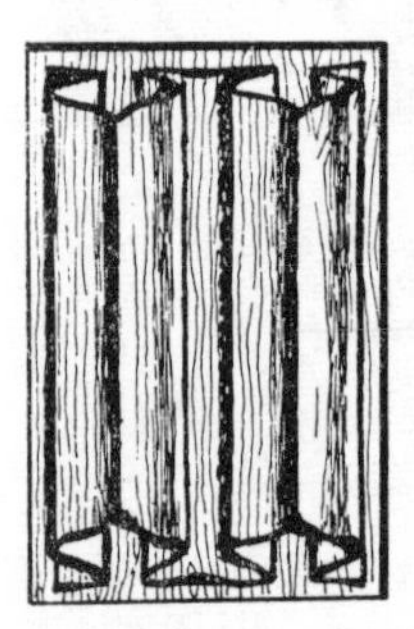

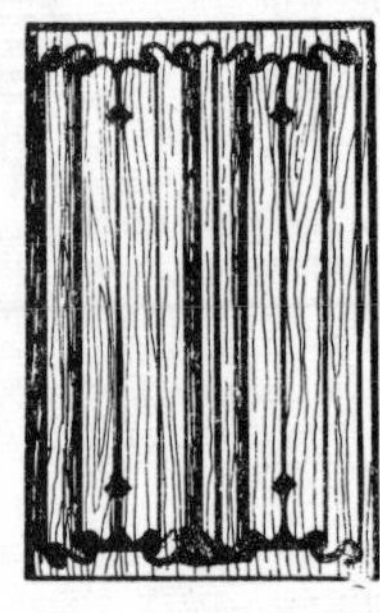

Fig. 13: Two panels of carved 'linen fold'. Introduced to England during the second quarter of the sixteenth century and of Flemish origin, it was popular during the remainder of the century; extant contemporary English examples are fairly plain. It was much used for decoration during the Victorian age.

Inlay decoration was used in conjunction with carving, turning and, by the 1620s, the 'moulded front' on drawer, door and chest panels. As we have seen, the practice of carving the panels on the front and sides of furniture was by this time well established, and one consistently fashionable design during the sixteenth and early seventeenth centuries was the 'linen fold', see fig. 13. The panel is carved in low relief to give the appearance of a carefully folded piece of cloth solidified and applied to the panel, the effect of this being to raise or bring out the centre of the panel while the four sides recede into the framework. Continuing and elaborating on this raised effect was the moulded front, plate 5. The drawer was set back in the carcase frame, say, three-quarters of an inch. Four strips of wood were then applied round the edge forming a frame. The strips were of triangular section, and the longest side was moulded or grooved. Another piece of wood of the same proportions as the drawer front, but smaller, was then applied to the centre. This piece might be up to one and a half inches thick and was framed with more moulding; in the centre of this went the metal handle. The more elaborate chests of the 1620-1640 period had many complex variations on this symmetrical moulded theme. A typical example is the chest with one long deep drawer moulded to simulate two short drawers above two cupboard doors similarly decorated and enclosing three plain fronted drawers, plate 6. The two doors were secured by an iron lock and swung open on iron hinges. A substantial piece of moulding was then added immediately below the drawer or door opening at the base of the carcase to balance the overhanging top and the whole article was raised from the floor by the elongated upright members of the carcase.

By the early 1620s an improved method of joining the front panel to the sides of drawers had been devised, the back joints being secured with iron nails in the established manner. This method was known as 'dove-tailing' from the shape of the parts and counterparts to be joined, plate 3, and on the earliest or provincial examples of dovetailing the joints were strengthened with iron pins driven through the ends, also plate 3. However, the rapid advance of joiners' skill and the introduction of new materials during the following twenty years dispensed with the need for this nailing on the finest furniture, but it can sometimes be found on country-made pieces as late as the beginning of the eighteenth century, Plate 3.

Charles I, 1625-1649

Charles I, unlike James I, had immense personal influence on style and fashion, and was responsible for many of the revolutionary changes in our pattern of living. His marriage to Henrietta, daughter of Henry IV of France, increased continental influence on design, fashion and etiquette. Charles I was not only a connoisseur and a patron of art, he was the first recognised collector of works of art from other countries as well as England. He was fond of and advocated reading, hitherto confined to lay scholars and the clergy, and he encouraged the development of trade with Europe and the Middle and Far East through our own East India Company. This company had been incorporated by Royal Charter in 1600 to compete with the Dutch merchants for trade in lands beyond the Cape of Good Hope or the Straits of Magellan. Thus began an age of great commercial expansion.

We were importing fine porcelain from China, glass from Venice, pottery from Delft in Holland, spices and peppers from the East Indies, fine cloth from Damascus and Italy, chests or trunks from Japan decorated with the gum of the lac tree and known as Japanned work or lacquer, all of which were to have important influence on the development of English furniture. As the requirements of household furniture became rapidly more diverse, more accuracy was necessary in its manufacture, and coinciding with this was the more general use of walnut, much of which was imported from Spain and the south of France. Walnut, which until the latter part of the seventeenth century was used in the solid, had a much closer grain than oak, and could therefore be cut more exactly. When rubbed well down by hand polishing it showed great depth of colour and extremely attractive markings. By this time we were beginning to use imported fabric and fine leather to cover the seats and backs of chairs. Apart from the Court and wealthier households, covered chairs were generally regarded as bedroom articles, being too costly for the rigours of everyday use. The examples of covered chairs of the Charles I period that can be said to have been designed for use outside the bedroom are those of square and solid shape, and with a low back. This was to accommodate the arm of the gentleman as he sat sideways, encumbered by his sword. The practice of leaving personal armament in the anteroom did not start until the early eighteenth century. Also the back legs of chairs had, during this period, become permanently splayed out to counteract the inborn habit of all generations to tip back.

Although we were covering chairs with various fabrics, upholstery, i.e. padding and stuffing before covering, was rare before 1645 and it was to become even more rare in the immediate future. We had begun to experiment and expand in many fields—trade, commerce, sacred and secular architectural design, exploration—when the country was divided by the Civil War. This outwardly ended with the execution of Charles I and the exile to France of his two sons, Charles and James. The eleven year Commonwealth which followed, under the rule of Oliver Cromwell, 1649-1660, was a period of overriding religious zeal, and the development and advancement of design was curbed.

Commonwealth, 1649-1660

Puritan beliefs of this period decreed righteouness in self-denial, and furniture made in the Midlands and south of England during the Commonwealth reflects this feeling. The 1650s were notoriously dull years as far as furniture is concerned, and everything that could be associated with gracious living was discouraged. All goods and chattels were made to be strictly functional, without unnecessary adornment, with precious little comfort, and lacking in artistic sensibility.

But at least two men during this period were working on experiments that were to create new exercises for the skills of our craftsmen in the near future. As early as 1643 Evangelista Torricelli, while working on a theory by Galileo, had discovered that the external atmosphere controls the power of a vacuum inside a sealed tube. If a glass tube has a measured amount of mercury—a non-evaporative liquid—poured into it and is then sealed, the rise and fall of the mercury will indicate the external atmosphere or barometric pressure. Torricelli was unfortunately hampered by the lack of sufficiently advanced materials, the most important being suitable glass tubing, but we were well on the way to the first domestic barometer. The other man was Christian Huygens, a Dutchman, who in 1657 discovered the importance of the applied pendulum. This was originally yet another of Galileo's theories, but he had used it only in the research of oscillations. By giving a pendulum momentum by means of power from a weight on a chain or specially woven rope over a toothed wheel and correcting the length of the arc of its swing by means of a mechanical escapement, it was possible to achieve accuracy with a timepiece movement. Thus began the development of the clock, which soon became popular in the finer houses all over England, see fig. 14.

Restoration and Carolean, 1660-1685

Charles II landed at Dover in May, 1660, and was crowned at Westminster in April, 1661. In 1662 he married Catherine of Braganza. He was quick witted, a man of great and varied knowledge, and a shrewd judge of men. From Holland he

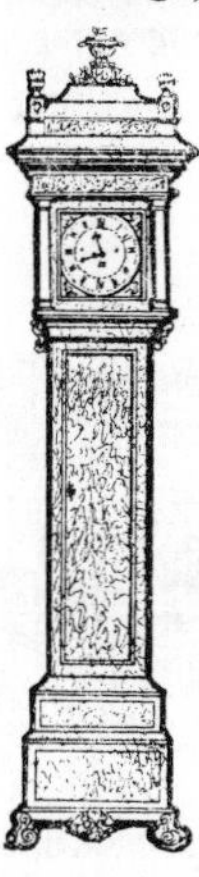

Fig. 14: A walnut veneered long case clock, c. 1700. This artist's impression is intended to show the elaborate extremes achieved by cabinet makers for this relatively new household article by 1700. By this time cases of the same outline but with less ornate decoration were being made in various parts of Britain. From 1695 to 1720 marquetry, and from 1700 to 1725 lacquer work, were popular types of decoration for clock cases.

brought a mistress—Louise de Kerouaille—who later became the Duchess of Portsmouth, and in England he found Nell Gwynn. He loved his children, his dogs, his ducks and his Navy. He enjoyed theatre-going, horse racing and gambling, while at the same time patronising the arts and encouraging further trade with Europe and the East. The best social and court biographies of this period are the diaries of Samuel Pepys, but the inclusion here of a brief mention of some of Charles II's interests illustrates one reason why so many innovations in the design and uses of furniture came to be crammed together in such a short period. What Charles patronised in social life, his courtiers, the noblemen, landed gentry and so on down the social scale followed as far as their means would allow. A general interest in the arts developed. People started collecting china, pottery and glass. As these collections grew, and clocks and barometers became more fashionable, a new type of furniture was needed to house them—case and cabinet furniture. With the import of

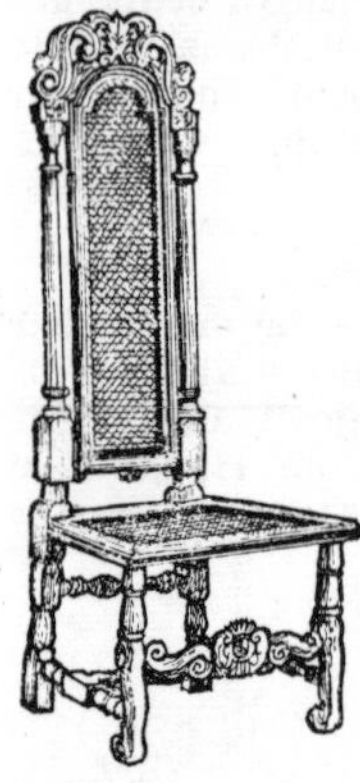

Fig. 15: A walnut framed cane panel chair typical of the James II period. The tall narrow back with the cane panel between turned supports was popular after 1685 until the end of the century. The variety of foreign designs appearing in England at this time was incorporated in crestings, stretchers, rails, legs and back supports, making this type of chair particularly interesting and possible to date with accuracy.

Fig. 16: A chair rail of bow form of the 1680s, shown here with the scroll or Braganza foot. During this period, the H stretcher on this type of frame chair was sometimes replaced by an elaborate curving X.

glass from Venice (and one or two highly prized secrets concerning its manufacture) it became obvious that the panels in the doors of cupboards should be of glass instead of wood, thus displaying the prized collections at the same time as protecting them from dust and breakage. The old method of joining and allowing room for the wood to 'move' proved inadequate for glass panels, which did not need to expand and contract, and therefore frames had to be constructed with joints cut to a higher degree of accuracy. The demand for case furniture became so great that a new craftsman emerged, a man specialising in the manufacture of case and cabinet furniture—the cabinet maker.

In 1663, George Villiers, second Duke of Buckingham, secured the sole right to manufacture mirror plates of silvered glass which he unjustly claimed was a process hitherto unknown in England. He started a factory at Vauxhall, and brought over glassmakers from Italy, then the centre of the glass industry, but his discovery was soon to affect the craftsmen of England. Several other patents and monopolies appear to have been granted at the same time, and as the output of mirror glasses grew so did the need for decorative frames to surround them. Many materials were used, such as metal, ivory, tortoiseshell and even needlework over a wood base, but the most popular to emerge was the wood frame intricately pierced and cut by the carver and later decorated by the gilder, see page 25 and plate 7.

During the 1660s we began importing large quantities of cane from the East, which when woven and strung across the open

Fig. 17: An oak settle of plain panelled construction. These were made in the provinces in this form from the second quarter of the seventeenth century throughout the eighteenth century. Without much decoration, accurate dating of this type of article can be difficult.

seats and backs of chairs provided a greater degree of comfort. Fine examples of cane panel seat furniture made during the last quarter of the seventeenth century can still be found today, see plate 8. Perhaps the most common is the high back walnut chair which can be used as either a dining or hall chair, see fig. 15, and which underwent such severe changes in shape as to make it possible to date accurately during the ensuing twenty-five years. The 'H' stretcher frame for chairs became really popular during the early Restoration period, the cross member being slightly more to the front on later examples. Pierced carving on the back top and side rails also became popular, and was adopted for the decoration of the Dutch bow front rail during the 1680s, see fig. 16. A direct influence from Holland where Charles had spent much of his exile was the Flemish curve which started to appear on the front legs of furniture, especially chairs. This was often combined with the scroll foot, see fig. 16, known as the 'Braganza Foot', a Spanish influence honouring the Queen.

There were many influences on English design during the Charles II period, with Dutch, Spanish and French appearing from the Continent and, following the great popularity of the merchandise brought over by the East India Company, our first period of 'Chinoiserie'. One reason for the tremendous output of fashionable furniture at this time was the devastating Great Fire of London in September 1666, when 13,200 houses were burnt to the ground. As these were gradually rebuilt, so they were refurnished in the fashionable styles of the day. By the 1670s walnut was considered the standard material for all the finest quality furniture, and our cabinet makers were called upon to manufacture glazed door cabinets, blind (solid wood or mirror plate) door cabinets, cases for clocks and barometers and escritoires; the joiners were producing a new and large variety of tables each for a specific use; and the chair makers and turners were making chairs, day-beds and settles, see fig. 17. The day-bed, derived from the French chaise-longue, first appeared in England during the early Restoration period. It was made in the same manner as the contemporary chairs, but with a seat that extended forward some five feet, see fig. 18.

Fig. 18: An early Restoration period day bed, c. 1660. Day beds were introduced in England during the first half of the sixteenth century and had become popular by the early 1600s. After the Restoration, their design closely followed that of the chair, and changes in shapes of chairs can safely be said to apply to day beds of the same period.

Fig. 19: A writing desk or escritoire c. 1695. The two inside front legs swing out and support the sloping 'fall' which is hinged at the bottom front edge. During the early eighteenth century, the box part was placed on a chest of drawers base to make what is now known as a bureau.

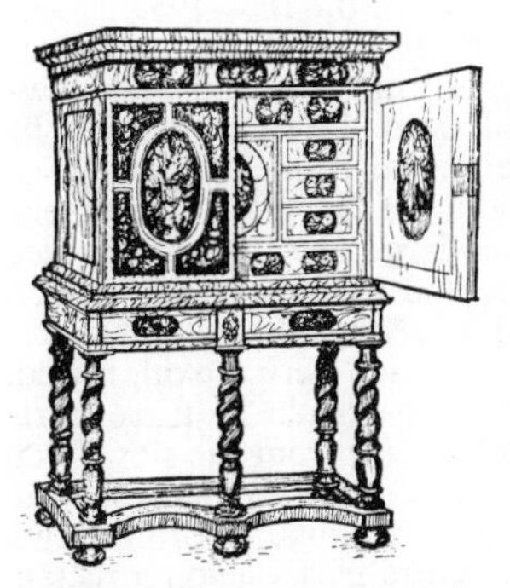

Fig. 20: A Charles II type of cabinet on stand, c. 1675. Panels of marquetry decorate the door and drawer fronts. Similar decoration was often used on the escritoire cabinet of the period where the two doors are replaced by one large one hinged at the bottom and which opens down to form a writing surface. The semi-circular or oval moulding below the top conceals one long 'secret' drawer.

Through its construction, however, it was not very practicable or long-lasting, and those examples that remain today are not really strong enough for daily use.

During the reign of Charles II the demand grew for smaller articles of furniture made for a specific purpose. One example is the escritoire. A development of the early desk with a sloping top and a forerunner of the bureau, the escritoire was rare in England before the middle of the seventeenth century, but its considerable use is recorded after the Restoration. Basically formed as a desk with a space to accommodate the knees of the writer, and in some instances with a flap that folded in half to form a larger surface, a small drawer was often incorporated in the frieze of the stand, see fig. 19. The design of the stand inevitably followed the latest developments in the art of the turner. One such development during the Charles II period was the 'barley sugar twist' turning. This design, which is self-descriptive, remained popular in the provinces until well into the eighteenth century, but it had disappeared from the manufacture of fashionable furniture by the early 1700s, see plate 8. Early barley sugar twist turning was a difficult operation for seventeenth century turners. Largely responsible for much refinement in this craft was the development of the sliding rest. This was a device which enabled the turner to rest his hand and turning chisel on a bracket which slid along parallel with the piece of wood to be turned. Imagine a circular piece of wood mounted in a lathe, and a line gouged along its length from left to right. If the wood had been rotated while the line was being gouged, the result would be a line encircling the wood from end to end. The speed the gouge is drawn from one end to the other together with the speed of the lathe determines the length of the spiral, and either heavy or fine barley sugar turning is produced. This type of turning formed the legs and stretchers of many of the gate leg tables and chairs of the 1660-1685 period, as well as the supports for the chests and cabinets-on-stands which were becoming so popular during this time. A chest containing perhaps a dozen small deep drawers enclosed by two large doors was placed on an open framed stand which might have had a drawer in the frieze, see Fig. 20. Alternatively, the two doors were replaced by one large one that was hinged at the bottom instead of the sides, and so fell down and out, making a writing surface supported by chains or steel arms.

During the early years of the Restoration period oval, round, rectangular and square tables with tops made in three parts became popular. These were a development from the single flap tables of about 1620. The two outside pieces or 'leaves' were attached to the centre with simple iron hinges, folding down when not in use, see plate 12. The centre part was on a rectangular frame with a leg at each corner and a square frame set in each long side. This swung out on a pivot joint from the main rectangle and, having its then outside upright member the same length as the four main legs, served to support the drop leaf. The name gate-leg has been used to describe this type of table for many years because of its construction, but not all tables of this period had a complete framed 'gate'.

Having dealt briefly with the continental effects on our furniture history, it is advisable to consider the work of the carver and gilder and also the Chinoiserie style in some detail, as all three recur and will be referred to again during the eighteenth and nineteenth centuries. See charts on pages 194 and 195.

The potential skills of the carver developed with the continuance of the use of walnut as seen in the fret or through cutting and shaping on the chairs of the period. But his work

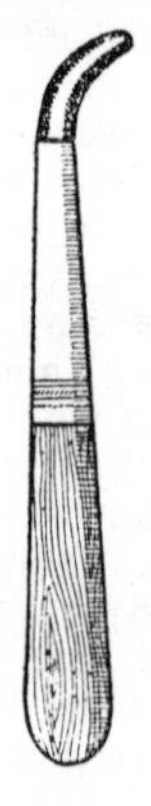

Fig. 21: An agate polisher. This highly polished semi-precious stone replaced for the most part the original dog's tooth used by gilders in England once the decoration of furniture with metal leaf became popular during the latter part of the seventeenth century. It was used to burnish and produce highlights after the gold or silver leaf had been applied.

was even more in demand with the fashion for gilding the surface of carved furniture. As the carved wood was to be covered there was no need to use walnut, and cheaper and softer woods could be used. Pine and lime were found to be excellent for the carvers' work and also for the application of a formula known as gesso prior to the application of the gold or silver leaf itself.

Gesso, which is a combination of pure fine chalk and size made from scrapings of parchment mixed together to make a paste, had been applied to the surface of furniture as a 'grain-filler' prior to decoration since the Middle Ages, but during the seventeenth century its full potential in the hands of a skilled carver became appreciated. The deep open carving was coated with several layers of gesso, each being allowed to dry before the application of the next. This then formed a surface as hard and, when well rubbed down, as smooth as ivory. The carver could then accentuate his work by carving further fine detail into the gesso itself before the article was sent to the gilder. Several coats of burnish size were applied and allowed to harden before the gilder wet the surface with water and then applied the pure gold leaf. As the burnish size quickly absorbed the moisture only small areas could be gilded at one time, thus making the achievement of a consistent colour and surface on large pieces a highly skilled and lengthy process. When the whole had been covered with gold it was rubbed well with a pad, making the surface dull or 'matt'. It was then ready for the finishing stage. Important and often protruding parts of the carving were burnished to a mirror-like surface, thus gaining the 'highlights'. This was done with a dog's tooth or later a polished agate stone correctly shaped and set into a convenient handle, see fig. 21. The two main methods of gilding furniture are water gilding, described above, and oil gilding. The latter is used more architecturally and on internal and external iron-work and cannot be burnished. It is cheaper, requires less painstaking surface preparation and is generally considered inferior for fine furniture decoration. Fire or mercurial gilding had been used to decorate metals since the Middle Ages. Fine silverware and, during the seventeenth, eighteenth and early nineteenth centuries, metal mounts for furniture were gilded in this way. Mercury and gold will mix and form an amalgam; this is applied to the surface of the metal and the article is then heated. The mercury evaporates and leaves a gold coating. This method is no longer used in England, for the fumes from evaporating mercury are extremely dangerous.

The Chinoiserie taste of the Carolean period made itself apparent in furniture with the considerable use of Japanned or lacquered decoration. Originating in the East, both panels and complete articles of lacquered furniture were imported to this country in vast quantities. To combat this it became expedient that a similar form of decoration should be produced over here. But while we could import as much lacquer work as we wanted, we could not obtain the essential ingredients to make the lacquer, nor had we the right climate or temperament for its application, so the English craftsmen started to copy it as best they could. In 1688, John Stalker and George Parker produced a *Treatise of Japanning and Varnishing*, an important and comprehensive work giving full directions and details concerning surface decoration of furniture. Instead of gum from the lac tree, we used a variety of varnishes and other materials which, it was found, could be turned to considerable advantage. Whereas the background of seventeenth century Oriental lacquer was invariably black, English lacquer of the same period was produced with red, yellow, green and blue backgrounds. The appearance of Japanned work is of scenes wherein the figures, birds, flowers and other main characters are slightly raised from the background surface and then decorated with colour and/or gold leaf.

The methods of making and applying both English and Oriental lacquer are highly technical and space does not allow a comprehensive account in this text, but the fact that the two methods were different has, over the years, presented us with a guide to distinguishing one from the other. During a life span of two hundred and fifty years it is inevitable that the outer surface of lacquer furniture has suffered some damage. Where

Fig. 22: An example of a lacquer cabinet on stand of the first Chinoiserie period, c. 1685. Cabinets of this period were either of Oriental origin and purchased through the East India Company at sales held on the docksides of London, or made in England and decorated in imitation by craftsmen and amateurs. The stands were made in England of carved pine, treated with gesso and then applied with metal leaf. See Gesso and Lacquer.

seventeenth century English lacquer has chipped and come away from the surface, it has done so in the outline of the raised parts, making obvious the shape and size of the character now missing. Oriental lacquer of the same period tends to come away in irregular sized pieces.

Both English and Oriental lacquer cabinets, enclosed chests and trunks were popular in England until the early 1700s, and the later ones were often placed on specially made carved and gilt wood stands. See fig. 22.

At the Court of Charles II, gambling had become a fashionable pastime, so the gaming table became one of the new types of furniture required of the joiner. During the last quarter of the seventeenth century card games of loo, basset, ombre and quadrille (ombre for four) were played for high stakes, as well as chess, backgammon and dicing. Card games were played best on tables covered with green cloth or fine needlework. Partly to protect this the tables were made to fold over in half, one or two legs being made to swing out from the frame in the manner of the earlier gate to support the top when open. Also, when closed the table showed a solid wood surface and could stand against the wall to be used as an additional side table. During this period, the East India Company began importing large quantities of chaw, or tea as it is now called, from China. In 1679 the Duchess of Lauderdale is recorded as having a gathering of ladies to sample her chaw in the withdrawing room at Ham House, being probably the first 'tea party', and naturally a table was specially made on which to present the tea. Inevitably the high price of tea at this time kept it within the reach only of the wealthy, and so tea drinking did not seriously affect the designs of furniture until the end of the seventeenth and early part of the eighteenth centuries.

In 1674 George Ravenscroft patented a tough clear glass which essentially founded the domestic glass industry in this country and was to affect furniture in many ways, particularly in the production of barometers and their cases, for it was found that the glass could be drawn into a hollow tube with a one-tenth inch bore. Following the work of Torricelli, Sir Samuel Morland produced in 1670 a signpost barometer, see fig. 23. The bend in the tube extends about twelve inches and rises off the horizontal about three inches, thereby showing with greater accuracy any atmospheric change along rather than up and down the tube. This type did not gain the popularity expected and the stick or pillar type of case continued to be made with its decoration following the styles of the different periods for the next two hundred years, see fig. 24. It was superseded in general popularity toward the end of the eighteenth century by the banjo

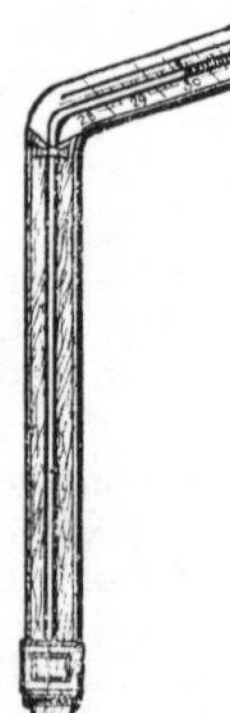

Fig. 23: A signpost barometer. First used in England by Sir Samuel Morland about 1670, the signpost barometer gave greater accuracy of reading 'along' the tube rather than up and down as on the vertical type. However, it never gained the popularity of the vertical or stick barometer though it continued to be made throughout the eighteenth century, its case following to some degree the current designs.

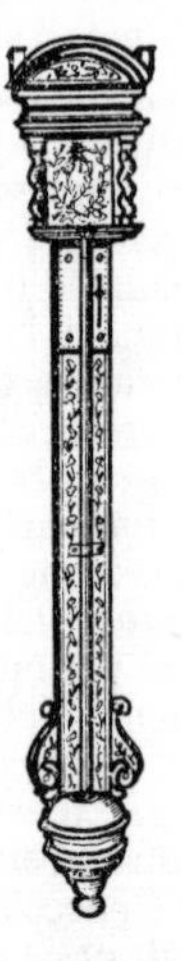

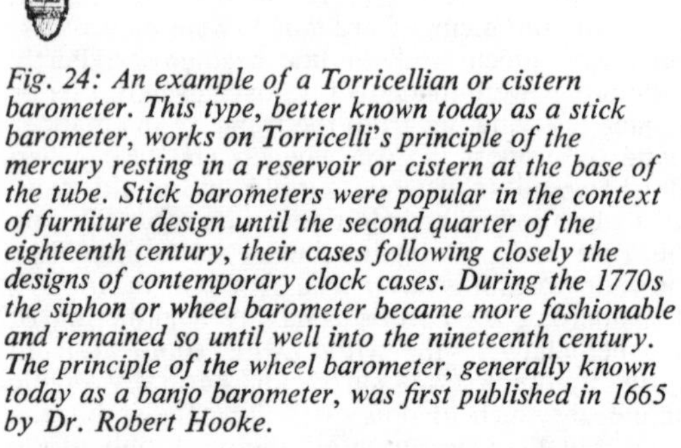

Fig. 24: An example of a Torricellian or cistern barometer. This type, better known today as a stick barometer, works on Torricelli's principle of the mercury resting in a reservoir or cistern at the base of the tube. Stick barometers were popular in the context of furniture design until the second quarter of the eighteenth century, their cases following closely the designs of contemporary clock cases. During the 1770s the siphon or wheel barometer became more fashionable and remained so until well into the nineteenth century. The principle of the wheel barometer, generally known today as a banjo barometer, was first published in 1665 by Dr. Robert Hooke.

or wheel barometer, but returned to favour during the latter part of the nineteenth century.

During the reign of Charles II domestic architecture became a distinct profession; one which had been started in the classical traditions by Inigo Jones (1573-1652) during the first half of the seventeenth century, and which was to affect our furniture design through the work of Daniel Marot during the late seventeenth century and William Kent in the first part of the eighteenth century. Just as real development in all branches of the constructive arts and skills was taking place throughout the country we entered a short period of political unrest and turmoil.

James II, 1685-1689

James II, the second son of Charles I, and his Court had no direct influence on the designs of furniture. Politically he undid much of the good that Charles II had achieved and seemed to have learnt little from the fate of his father. Without direct influence the development of design was for a short time left to the craftsmen. Chair backs were made higher and tended to show a preference for baluster and vase turning, especially on the outside upright members. The seats became narrower, the spaces between the caning became smaller and the work much finer. Otherwise the basic shapes of furniture remained without any significant change and the industry might well have stagnated had we not had an injection of impetus with craftsmen from the Continent. The Revocation of the Edict of Nantes in 1685 deprived the Huguenots (French Protestants) of all civil and religious rights and liberty, and they were forced to flee the country and find sanctuary in Holland and the British Isles. The Huguenots were industrious and highly skilled. They brought to this country new standards of manufacture in woodwork and metalwork (see *Discovering Hall Marks on English Silver*) and new techniques in the weaving of cloth suitable for upholstery. Previously only fine brocades and velvets from Italy and, during the Commonwealth, leather had been used to cover the seats and backs of chairs, but because of their formidable cost and in the case of leather comparative lack of comfort, only on a very small scale. The Government encouraged the weaving of fabric in this country and although the Upholders (later Upholsterers) Guild had been formed prior to 1460, it was not until the end of the seventeenth century that the use of fabric for decoration and comfort and the upholsterer became integral parts of our furniture history.

William and Mary, 1689-1702

The next important development in furniture decoration came with the accession to the throne of England of William III and his wife, Mary II, daughter of James II. William was the son of William, Prince of Orange, who had married Mary, daughter of Charles I. After considerable discontent throughout England with the reign of James II, and following a brief interregnum from 11th December, 1688, to 13th February, 1689, William and Mary were invited to come over from Holland and rule England jointly, the affairs of state being left to William alone. With a Dutch king we naturally had still more influence in our design from the Continent, and with a reigning queen, court and social behaviour again affected the manners and habits of the people. William III brought with him craftsmen skilled in the art of furniture manufacture and we can see evidence of this Dutch influence in both the shape and decoration of much of the better quality household furniture of this post Restoration period. The method of enhancing furniture with thin slices of wood fixed to the surface of the carcase or main body of an article was known as early as the second quarter of the seventeenth century, but it really became popular in England during the 1690s. Now known as veneer it was originally called 'faneer'

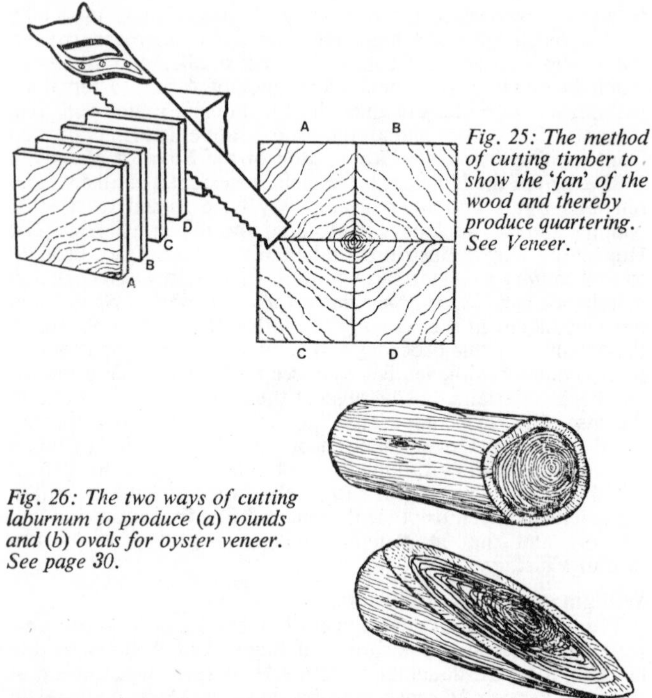

Fig. 25: The method of cutting timber to show the 'fan' of the wood and thereby produce quartering. See Veneer.

Fig. 26: The two ways of cutting laburnum to produce (a) rounds and (b) ovals for oyster veneer. See page 30.

because the slices were cut across the grain of the wood thus showing the 'fan' of the timber, fig. 25, rather than with the grain, a practice which became popular during the eighteenth century. The term veneer today encompasses the many variations on a theme which quickly developed. Some types were extremely popular for a limited period to be revived at a later date while others continued throughout the eighteenth and nineteenth centuries to the present day. Of the former oyster-shell parquetry and marquetry are the two most important examples. It was found that not only walnut, which was now being imported from France as well as Spain, but also laburnum wood were ideal for veneer. The branches of laburnum were cut at an angle to give oval shapes (oysters) and straight across to give round ones, see fig. 26. Sometimes the outer ring of sapwood was retained to enhance the oysters of rounds which were then arranged so as to form regular patterns on the surface of the article to be decorated. Interspersing these patterns were lines of box wood, about one-eighth of an inch square in section, known as stringing. Parquetry also applies to any veneering where pieces of wood of contrasting colours are cut and laid so as to form a geometric or symmetric pattern.

The use of marquetry in the form it took during the late seventeenth century was the direct result of the influence of the skills of the Dutch craftsmen. Although a progression from the early type of crude inlay on the carcase to the achievement of this effect with veneers would no doubt have occurred in England anyway, it is accepted that during the reign of William and Mary the latter reached supreme heights of perfection, and the process of decoration known as marquetry became extremely popular.

The basic method of marquetry production is that a number of pieces of veneer cut wood of contrasting colours were glued together one on top of the other with a piece of paper in between each. A piece of rough wood was then placed on the two outer surfaces of the resultant 'sandwich' and on to one of these was pasted a sheet of paper bearing the design of the panel required. The pattern was then cut through with a fine saw blade set at exact right angles to the timbers, the two pieces of rough wood receiving the fraying action of the saw. When the design had been fully cut the woods were separated, using water and a thin bladed knife to work away the paper between each slice. Say four woods were used, there were now four panels, each with a design which could be replaced by three other colours. As walnut was the most popular background, not all the panels were utilised but were kept to be used in the event of breakages in subsequent repeats of the same design. There are two main types of marquetry, being classified as floral and arabesque or seaweed. The first, which is the earlier of the two, incorporated the use of acanthus leaf scrolls, vines, flowers and occasionally birds—parrots or eagles—set in panels surrounded by borders of stringing and crossbanding of walnut or kingwood. For this type a great variety of woods was used. Some were dyed to give additional colours, others were used in their natural state, sometimes being scorched by dipping in hot sand to give a shaded effect to the flowers and leaves, see plate 13. Further naturalistic effects on flower petals and leaves were obtained by saw cuts which were accentuated by the glue forced through to the surface during the application of the panel to the article of furniture. The practice of engraving the marquetry did not become popular until its revival during the latter part of the eighteenth century. Some of the woods used for natural colour were rosewood, sandal wood, orange and citron, while the lighter effects came from box, holly (the lightest), acacia and sycamore. Most other fruit woods were used and the background was generally walnut. Arabesque or seaweed marquetry, which was sometimes used in conjunction with parquetry, utilised only two woods; box or holly for the pattern and walnut for the background. The patterns were of the finest symmetrical scrollwork, demanding the highest possible degree of skill from the marquetry cutter and relying on the fineness of the work rather than an assortment of colours for its impact.

A type of veneering which was introduced during this period and remained popular well into the 1720s was a method known as quartering, see fig. 25. It was found that four slices of veneer cut from the same piece of wood naturally had almost identical markings. Although seventeenth and eighteenth century veneers were almost one-eighth and not less than one sixteenth of an inch thick, four slices could be produced by a good veneer cutter or sawyer from well under an inch of timber, allowing for the thickness of the saw. It was also found that the knots, burrs, growths and other irregularities on a tree produced the most attractive veneer. Imagine a cube of timber from which four cuts of veneer have been taken. If, say, the bottom left-hand corners are placed together when the four are laid out to form a large square, the pattern in the wood is not only repeated four times but joins itself at the edges. This method of decoration was employed all over the country, and some charming examples of attractive quartering on country-made furniture, the underneath or inside of which is often very poor quality, can still be found. Incorporated with and finishing off all types of veneering were the stringing, crossbanding and mouldings. Crossbanding is a decorative strip or line of veneer of variable width wherein the grain runs across the line and, during the walnut period, was applied in lengths of seldom more than three to four inches. Taking the same cube of timber used to illustrate quartering, a slice is cut from one side, say half an inch thick. This is then laid flat and cut in the same way as veneer, see fig. 27.

An advancement on this was the introduction of feathering or herring-bone crossbanding. For this effect the first cut in the cube was made diagonally approximately one-quarter of an inch thick. Two slices of banding were then cut from this, and when being laid as veneer one was turned over thus producing the herring bone, see fig. 27. The mouldings on the drawer fronts of earlier furniture were now being ousted by the decorative use of veneer, and so the moulding was placed round the edge of the drawer opening on the carcase. This took the form of a raised crossbanding of semi-circular and later semi-oval section, and within a few years a groove was worked in the moulding giving a double semi-circular section, see plate 14.

1. A fine example of an oak five-board chest with single-plank top, mid 16th century. The carved decoration to the upper part of the front is typical of the period, as are the chip carved edges to the sides of the front and lid. All original hand-made nails are visible at intervals along the front and so too is the original iron lock plate.

2. An oak chest, c. 1600. The front is arcaded in typical Renaissance manner and decorated with carved roundels and flower stalks.

3. Country made walnut chest furniture, 1700-1720. Although the side runner on the carcase fitting into the deep rabbet in the drawer shown here had been superseded by bottom runners on fashionable furniture by the end of the 17th century, their use continued on provincial furniture for several years. The large double dovetail joint at the drawer front and the single nail are also typical of earlier construction but the fact that the joint is stopped or lapped, i.e. the side of the drawer does not come through to the front of the drawer to be concealed by the veneer, indicates manufacture after 1690. The double moulded cross-banding on the carcase suggests c. 1710 and the herring bone banding on the drawer confirms 1710-1720. The gilt brass and engraved escutcheon plate handle, which is original, is of the type used during the first quarter of the 18th century. The faint horizontal lines on the drawer front suggest that at some time the article has been repolished but as can be seen on the lower left-hand corner the veneer is at least twice as thick as its 19th century counterpart. See Fakes, page 184.

4. An early 17th century oak chest with panelled top and ends below double plank top. It would originally have had a drawer below the chest space, which would account for the unusual depth of panelling at each end and the rabbet visible on the inside of the left front leg, cut to accommodate the drawer runner. Chests from the Norfolk area often have the fronts decorated with formal crest-like carving at this time.

5. A cedar wood and oak chest, c. 1660. The raised geometric decoration on the front of the deep top drawer and the two doors below was most popular between c. 1650 and 1665, the austerity of the design lending itself to the general severity of the Commonwealth period. The application of split pillars suggests more freedom which came with the Restoration. At some time during the mid 18th century this chest had bracket feet added to bring it more up to date with contemporary furniture. Following its discovery in 1968, these were carefully removed to reveal the original feet formed by the stiles which continue through to the top.

6. The interior of the lower part of the chest illustrated in plate 5. The doors swing on iron hinges nailed to the main upright members, called stiles, which on furniture of this period also form the feet. Three long drawers enclosed by the doors are plain except for three blocks of timber simulating a muntin. The centre block has the door lock fastening, and the original iron drop ring handles are typical examples, applied in the correct manner as shown in fig. 86 on page 188.

7. A late 17th century carved and gilt mirror frame, showing considerable European influence in the design of the top cresting. The base incorporates the shell motif which remained popular on the plainer furniture of the Queen Anne period.

8. (Left) A walnut armchair of the early Restoration period, c. 1665. This example shows the use of pierce carving with scallop shells, formal foliage scrolls and flower heads on the front stretcher and the frame for the back panel of canework. This can be seen to be coarse, with large holes. By 1680 the caning was finer with small holes. The H stretcher rails and the fine quality barley sugar twist turning are also indicative of the Restoration period. The carving in low relief on the seat rails, front legs and arm terminals and caps makes this chair a fine example of the period.

9. (Right) A late 17th century chair with ebonised beechwood frame. The high back panel flanked by turned columns, the flamboyant cresting rail and stretcher rail and the exaggerated curve to the knee of each leg are all features typifying a good example of the period, c. 1690.

10. (Top right) The cresting rail of the chair shown in plate 9, illustrating the fine quality and depth of carving to be expected in a pedigree chair of this type. The combination of scrolls and formalised leaves within an architectural frame further illustrates fashionable design for chairs of this period.

11. (Centre right) The stretcher rail and front legs of the chair shown in plate 9. The pattern of the top cresting rail is repeated in slightly flattened form below the seat rail. The faceted scroll legs are fluted at the knee and foot and carved with pendants.

12. (Left) A small gate leg table, c. 1675. Since the first part of the 16th century small folding tables were known in England, and during the 17th century their advantages were fully recognised. Gate leg tables of all sizes were produced from the second quarter of the 17th century and followed the progress of the turners' designs. Thus they can be dated after the introduction of a particular design; thereafter accuracy is difficult, for such patterns tended to remain popular in the provinces long after they had gone out of fashion in the large towns. This example shows extremely good baluster, ball and ring or bobbin turning, but a fine example might have the rails and stretchers turned to match. A single peg joint is also visible on the outer leg of the gate and the feet are original.

13. An extremely fine example of floral marquetry applied to a small lace or ruffle box, c. 1680. The stringing, crossbanding and use of all the techniques described on page 31 are seen here. Especially important are the saw cuts through the wood to accentuate the veins of leaves, petals and feathers. The glue which was forced through when the panel was applied has blackened with age and added definition. The practice of scribing the surface after its application to achieve the same effect was not done in England until the latter part of the 18th century when marquetry had a revival. Also clearly visible is the shaded effect achieved by dipping each piece of wood into hot sand.

14. A walnut-veneered deal side table of the William and Mary period, c. 1700. This example illustrates the details described on page 32 and also shows the careful choice and matching of timber. The shaped apron suggests a slightly later date, and the inclusion of the elaborate X stretcher with this points to a country made piece, perhaps a few years out of period.

15. The underside of the table shown in plate 14. The rough hewn surfaces of its inner sides complement the theory of provincial origin. However, authenticity is unquestionable: the clean appearance of the top planks which, when the drawer is in place, would receive no handling; the darkened edge of the shaped apron from hand and finger grease (a white line here would indicate false staining perhaps sixty years ago); the slight darkening between the side rail and where the drawer side fits shows where some, but not much, dusty air has circulated; a marked darkening on the outer edges of the top; and the extreme reaches of the polishing cloth on the inside of the leg finish in just the right place. *See Fakes, page 180.*

16. (Left) An early 18th century wing armchair with walnut show-wood frame, c. 1720 (see caption to plate 21). The arm supports on this turn out and over in contrast to the arm supports on the chair in plate 20. This creates an additional scroll to the outline. Referred to as a 'C' scroll, it can be seen repeated on the inside upper part of each front leg.

17. (Centre right) Necessary replacements which may affect the value. The centre stretcher has been replaced and, although it is of good shape, the restorer has overdone the 'distressing' or intentional bruising in an attempt to conceal the replacement. The regularity of the bruises draws attention to the part in question and closer examination reveals the colour and quality of the wood to be inconsistent with the rest of the underframe.

18. (Bottom right) The left side of the armchair in plate 16, showing the underframe and a replacement back leg. Here too the uniform pattern of bruises may give grounds for suspicion, which in this case are confirmed by the new timber and clearly apparent turning marks resulting from a mechanical lathe. Genuine bruising and signs of wear can be seen on the side stretcher to have produced a most mellow effect.

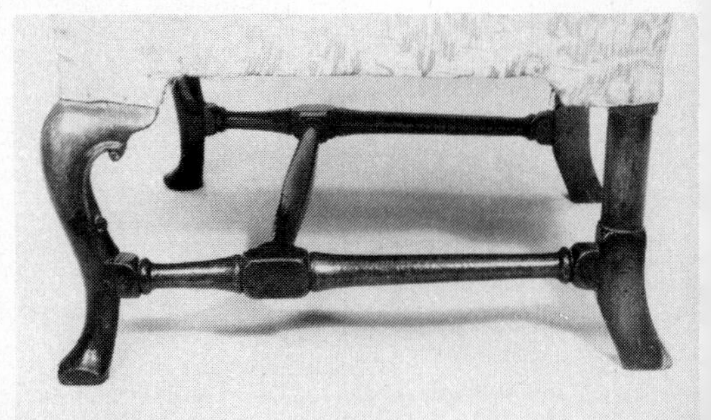

19. The new leg on the left lacks depth of colour and shows false shading. The black stain used to colour the leg has soaked into the fibres of the timber broken by the high speed machine lathe. The original leg on the right has no shading and no visible turning marks.

20. An early 18th century wing or 'easy' armchair, c. 1720, with walnut curved legs front and back terminating at front in pad feet and at back with square section. See fig. 33, A and B. Easy chairs with wings, or 'cheeks' as they were called, are recorded during the late 17th century but they did not become widely popular until the Queen Anne period.

21. (Left) A similar chair to the one shown in plate 20, but slightly later in period (c. 1745), showing the same lines and the method of construction. In the interests of economy, inexpensive timber was used for those parts of the framing of chairs which the upholstery would cover. Thus more costly mahogany legs and underframing can be seen here joined at the front and spliced at the back into the beech frame. Various restorers through the ages have strengthened the frame of this chair, noticeably at the top of the back and the front edge of the left wing, and the four brackets inside each corner of the frame are of a type not used until the 19th century. The original rope used by the upholsterer as an anchor is still retained on the inside of each wing.

22. (Right) An early George I period bureau cabinet. The top has open shelves with a row of small drawers at the bottom, all enclosed by two mirrored glass doors and surmounted by a flat cornice. Under each door in the cabinet section is a candle slide. The bureau has two short and two long drawers below a false or dummy drawer front which covers a space known as a well. Access to this is inside the sloping front of the bureau and is concealed by a sliding cover which when closed forms part of the writing surface immediately in front of the centre door compartment. The bureau is shown with the sloping front or 'fall' open to disclose the centre door compartment, a secret compartment each side hidden by simulated classical columns, pigeon holes and small drawers.

23. (Right) A fine example of a William and Mary period chest on stand. The underframe of six legs joined by a shaped stretcher typifies cabinet furniture of the late 17th century in one form or another and here shows the sturdy development from the more fragile barley sugar twist and generally taller stands of the 1660s and 1670s. The next development was to dispense with stretcher rails, as can be seen in plate 26.

24. (Left) A Queen Anne period kneehole desk or writing table, c. 1710. This clearly shows the two sets of three drawers and one long one framing the space to accommodate the knees of the user. The small simulated arch over is also a shallow drawer, and beyond this is a small cupboard with drawer under. All the features on this desk are original and contemporary. Note the bun feet, gilt metal handles and escutcheon plates, the semi-circular moulding at the base and the double moulding round the drawers.

25. (Left) A mahogany kneehole desk or writing table c. 1750-1755, showing the development from its prototype illustrated in plate 24. The drawers are shallower and the beading around each drawer front is attached to the drawer in the form of a cock bead rather than attached to the carcase as in the earlier period. The bun feet have gone out of fashion and square bracket feet are used instead.

!6. (Right) An early George I period walnut tallboy, c. 1715. The top three long and three short drawer chest with overhanging moulding stands in the original three drawer base on four curved cabriole legs erminating in pad feet. The herring bone banding has moved in from the edge of the drawer leaving a slightly larger margin for crossbanding, and the drawer fronts extend beyond the drawer opening. This pattern ran concurrently with inside drawers for some years, to be replaced by a cock bead during the 1730s.

27. (Right) A mahogany fold-over top card table, c. 1735. The frieze contains one long drawer which has the original escutcheon plate handle. The cabriole legs terminate in lion's paw feet, and the carved lion mask decoration at the knee can be seen to stand well proud of the outline of the curve.

28. (Left) A tripod base, rectangular top mahogany tea table, c. 1750. Examples of this period often have plain rectangular as well as circular tops: here can be seen the runners and block which enable the top to tip up but not revolve as in the case of a 'bird-cage' fitting. The carved square section of Rococo motif on the stem is particularly unusual. The writhen turned cup is above three decorated legs terminating in well formed ball and claw feet. Here too the carving can be seen to stand proud of the outline of the curve.

29. (Left) A mahogany tripod table, c. 1750. The pierced peg at the top of the column fits into a 'birdcage' which allows the table top to revolve and tilt, being secured with a wedge through the slot. The finely turned baluster-shape column has the lower part in a writhen turned cup which can be seen to stand proud of the outline of the curve. So too can the carved shell motifs on the knees. See also plate 66.

30. (Below) Tripod base kettle or urn stands. (Left) Mahogany, country made c. 1755, and interesting for the ringed tapering column, the inverted curved legs and the inclusion of small Gothic motifs at the base of the column. (Centre) Mahogany, country made c. 1755. The undecorated tapering or 'gun-barrel' column is out of period and more typical of country made pieces. Both these stands are too tall to have been made from pole screen bases, often a present-day hazard, and the proportions of the small tops on wide-spread bases compare favourably with right which is a Victorian version of a Gothic style stand; the inclusion of too many decorative features and poor proportions are the initial guides to the date of this piece. Also it is made of rosewood which makes it unlikely to have been made c. 1760 as its appearance might at first suggest. See also plates 102, 103 and 104.

31. (Left) A mahogany dumb-waiter of two tiers on tripod base, c. 1755. From the middle of the 18th century dumb-waiters developed in line with other tripod base occasional furniture, having three, four and even five tiers. Towards the end of the century these were sometimes made to drop down like the leaves of a pembroke table, being supported by a revolving bar. The tripod here shows a fine example of a plain curved leg terminating in a pad or club foot.

32. (Right) A later example of the mahogany dumb-waiter, c. 1790, with three instead of two trays, all of which revolve. An important feature of slightly later tripod tables is the disappearance of the pad foot and the use of the cap or toe castor to complete the end of the tapered leg.

33. (Left) A carved wood and gilt mirror, c. 1755. The frame clearly shows the 'C' scrolls combined with simulated rockwork and freely placed flowers. All are fine examples of typical Rococo decoration.

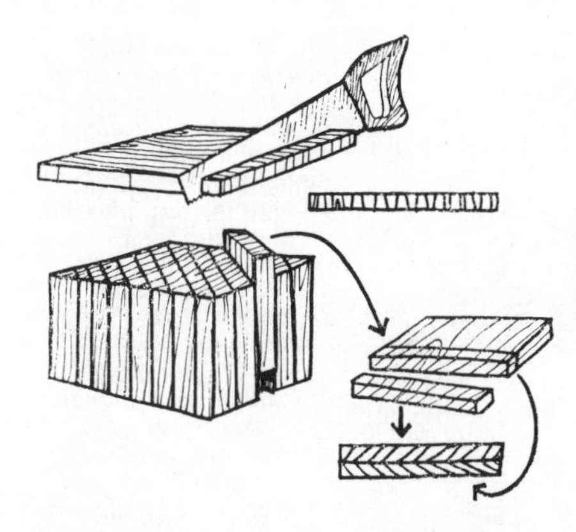

Fig. 27: The method of cutting timber to produce (top) crossbanding and (bottom) herring bone banding.

Almost without exception, herring-bone banding is peculiar to the period of walnut furniture in England, which ran from the Restoration period, from about 1660 to about 1730. The same might be said for crossbanded mouldings, but it must be remembered that fashion did not change overnight, and much furniture of the early mahogany period which began, in country furniture at least, about 1730, was produced with considerable influence of the previous period.

With the continued popularity of decorated furniture, whether lacquered, gilded or veneered, it was obvious that woods cheaper than oak might be used for the construction of the carcase or main body. Pine and deal were used to a great extent, and for veneered furniture especially the large flat surfaces required were formed by glueing planks of these woods side by side. Unfortunately, over the years it has become apparent how unsatisfactory this was, for being softer than oak, both these woods expand and contract to a greater degree and this method of construction gave them no room to do so. Hence the considerable amount of warping and cracking which can be a constant worry to those people lucky enough to own any genuine walnut period furniture today.

The next important development to begin during the late seventeenth century and which by the 1720s had altered forever the construction of our furniture was the production and use of metal screws. The tops of tables and chests which had previously been fastened by pegging through, were now screwed on from underneath. Incisions with a rounded surface were made in the inside of the top rail to accommodate the screw which went into the top at an angle, see fig. 28. The rounded surface of the incision should be noted, for it was not until the nineteenth

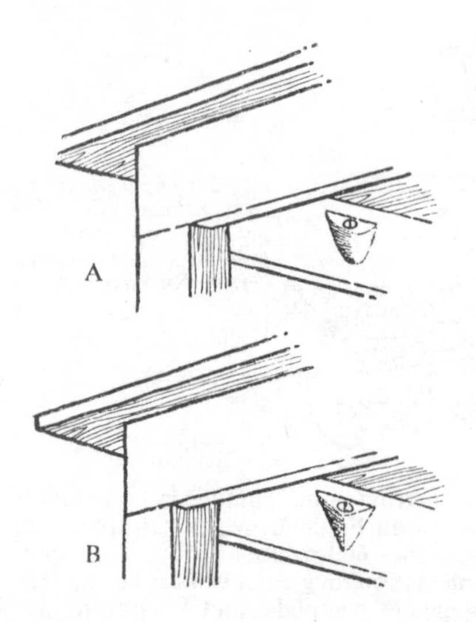

Fig. 28: (a) shows the rounded incision made to accommodate the screw securing the top on an eighteenth century piece of furniture. (b) shows the V shape incision adopted on English furniture during the latter part of the nineteenth century. During the eighteenth century many side, console and pier tables had marble tops; over the years these were often replaced with wooden tops which had to be screwed on. If the only incisions for screws in the underside of the frieze rail are V shaped the top is likely to have been fixed during the nineteenth century.

century that V incisions for this purpose were made on English furniture.

By the end of the seventeenth century the different articles of furniture in use in our middle and upper class houses had become as varied as the types of people who commissioned their manufacture. But one article in particular that had become standard household equipment was the tea table.

Although tea had been known in England since the early part of the seventeenth century, it was not until the late 1690s that it really began to affect our furniture industry. Tea was first noted in this country as having medicinal qualities, being a preventative against disease and a remarkable cure for hangovers. Naturally there were many who disapproved its use, viewing with disdain those high in social circles who had gained the habit of taking tea after dinner rather than a bottle and a pipe. Tea was shipped to this country in measures of a certain weight. The measure was a *kati* which equalled just over a pound avoirdupois, and so many containers each holding this weight were packed into chests for transportation. As the popularity of tea grew, so first the chests and then the *kati* boxes themselves became decorated. The *katis* were usually of tin, either lightly engraved in the Chinoiserie manner or Japanned. The early chests had hinged lids and were mostly covered with fine morocco leather and embellished with silver and/or gilt metal hinges, corners and locks.

Fig. 29: A rectangular tray top tea table in the style of the early eighteenth century. This type of table remained popular until the middle of the century when the tripod table gained favour.

Within a few years miniature chests made by the cabinet maker and containing up to three miniature *katis* for the home blending of the different sorts of tea being imported became increasingly popular. During the eighteenth century these small tea chests of single, double or triple compartments were made of all manner of materials by all manner of people. Toward the end of the eighteenth century the name changed from chest to 'caddy', derived from the original *kati.* Great ceremony was accorded to the drinking of tea, and despite its then prohibitive cost, it appears to have become very much a national habit by the end of the seventeenth century. In 1700 the Joiners' Company, in a case against the Import of Manufactured Furniture and Cabinet Work, complained that apart from the vast quantities of cabinets, chests, trunks, screens and chairs being unloaded at the Port of London by the East India merchants, over six thousand five hundred lacquered tea tables had been imported within the previous four years. A tax of 15% was subsequently put on all such merchandise, but the number shows just how popular tea drinking had become, and it is perhaps a reflection on the quality of the imported tea tables that apparently not one is known to have survived. The earliest examples of English made tea or china tables are rectangular with a dished or sunken top and, being intended for use in any part of the room, are equally decorated on all four sides, see fig. 29.

Before the end of the seventeenth century several other changes in the needs and uses of domestic furniture occurred which were to affect the furniture industry thereafter. One was the considerable use of the small single drawer side table. A typical example of a provincial or country-made side table of the William and Mary period is shown in plate 14. The crudely

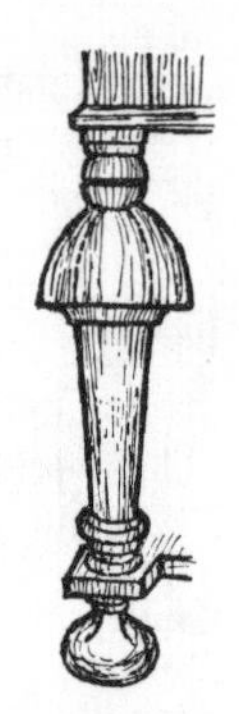

Fig. 30: The outline of the inverted cup turned pattern which had many decorated variations and was popular between 1690 and 1700.

made top of two rough hewn planks of deal (see plate 15) bears a finely quartered pegged-on top of matched walnut veneer incorporating the use of herring bone banding to frame the edges and create an oval in the centre. The outer edge is banded but not crossbanded, which was done to accentuate the crossbanding on the moulded lip. The drawer front and frieze are veneered through with walnut cut in the same way as oyster-shell, the line of the drawer being shown with a single band of herring bone banding. The frieze, even on most country furniture of this period, has become shaped. On contemporary chairs this shaped frieze effect was gained by the use of ornate and heavy fringes at the edges of the upholstery material which by now covered front and side rails as well as the seat. The shape of the stretcher illustrated is also similar to that of the chairs of the period, but a disappointing lack of decoration, under such a fine top, suggests the table was essentially a domestic article probably made for the servants' quarters in a fine house. The legs, too, might add weight to this supposition. Although the lower part with the straight tapering shape is all that could be desired, had the table been of great quality the top part would have had the inverted cup shape, see fig. 30, which required much larger pieces of timber for turning. The bun feet are also typical of this period, going out of fashion at the beginning of the eighteenth century.

Another similar type of table to become very popular at this time was the dressing or toilet table. Since as early as the fourteenth century both men and women had used considerable quantities of cosmetics and make-up, but it is unclear whether or not pieces of furniture were specially made to contain the numerous paints, powders, salves, hair dyes, perfumes, brushes, combs, etc. until the seventeenth century. However, during the late seventeenth century, when people actually died from applying too much make-up with a white lead or mercury base, toilet tables and toilet sets are specifically mentioned. Their design is similar to that of the side table until the 1720s, except that the single shallow drawer was narrower and extra space was provided by a deep drawer at each end accommodated in a more deeply shaped frieze, see fig. 31. From the beginning of the eighteenth century it was usual to have a dressing table made with a matching toilet mirror which stood on the top; this was a simply framed mirror plate connected to two upright supports by two swivel screws, and supported on a box type base containing one or two rows of small drawers, see fig. 32.

Fig. 31: A three drawer dressing table of the early eighteenth century type. The curved legs, shown here terminating in pad feet, should continue through to the top forming the corner stiles of the carcase frame and could be of solid oak, walnut, or after 1725, mahogany.

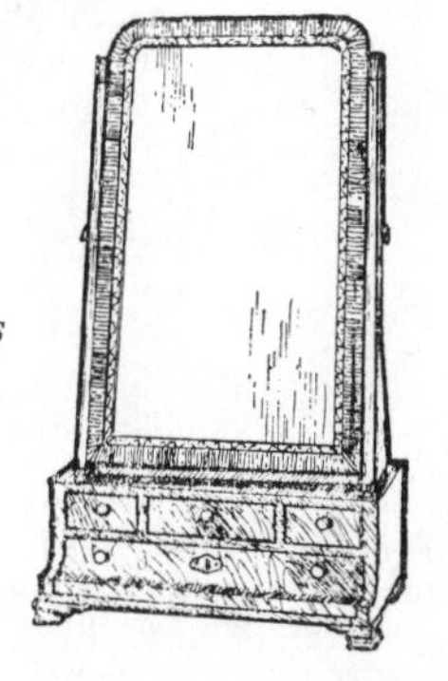

Fig. 32: A walnut period box base toilet mirror, 1710. The crossbanded frame has a narrow gilt inside border and swings on two fixing screws. This shape of base, sometimes with a single row of drawers, or a single drawer, was popular throughout the first half of the eighteenth century.

The furniture industry was to expand and flourish in an age of a complex pattern of fashions and designs sometimes changing rapidly, sometimes running concurrently. It was encouraged by the growth of population, internal prosperity and technical advancement and unrestrained by political and religious influence. It was also an age of trade publications. Leading manufacturers and designers produced and sold books of their designs which were copied by craftsmen throughout the land as well as their skill, materials available and the money at their disposal would allow. The pattern had been set during the reign of William III by his designer, Daniel Marot. In 1684, the year before the Revocation of the Edict of Nantes, Daniel Marot, a Huguenot, left his native France to seek asylum in Holland. He was already well known as an architect and furniture designer and before long was working for William, Prince of Orange. In 1694 Marot came to England and continued working under the royal patronage. He is probably best known for his designs of corner chimney pieces with graduated shelves above, but these were only one example of his adaptations from the heavy and ornate Louis XIV style. A book of Daniel Marot's designs published in the early eighteenth century shows considerable use of elaborate drapery for curtains, bed hangings, chairs and stools. His designs for the 'show wood' parts of furniture advocate much ornate carving with amorini or cherubs, masks, torsos and figures, at the same time incorporating many of the patterns already mentioned such as the bow or hoop stretcher rail, the inverted cup and straight taper turning and the curved front leg, see fig. 33A.

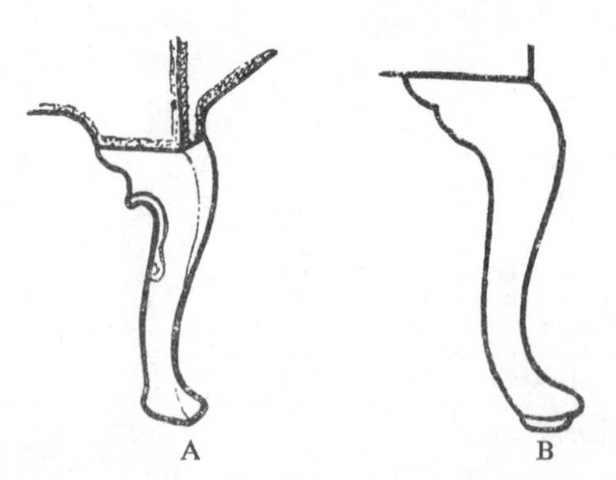

Fig. 33: The curved leg, introduced and becoming popular in England during the early eighteenth century. The square section foot (a) *preceded the round pad foot* (b) *but continued with it until 1725.*

THE EARLY EIGHTEENTH CENTURY

Queen Anne, 1702-1714

Two years after the turn of the century, William III died and Anne, second daughter of James II, succeeded to the throne in her thirty-seventh year. She was a thoroughly good woman, gentle, amiable and kind. Hers was the period of great victories on the Continent—we were once again at war with France—under the leadership of John Churchill, Duke of Marlborough. His wife Sarah Jennings was also an important figure, for she had considerable influence over the Queen. It was an age of great statesmen and great men of literature, and in 1706-7 the final Union of England and Scotland. In our furniture history we had the beginning of a combination of comfort and elegance in general middle class articles. For the first time the backs of chairs were shaped in solid wood to fit the body of the sitter.

Fig. 34: A walnut chair in the style popular from 1710 to c. 1730. The solid wood back splat is shaped for added comfort. The generous sweep of the back frame is apparent in the arms and was often repeated in the shape of the seat frame. Stretcher rails are rarely found on chairs of this pattern, but reappeared on fashionable furniture after the 1750s.

A large centre splat of stylised vase shape was supported by a curved frame, and the seat frame continued this shape by ballooning out towards the front, see fig. 34. Fully upholstered wing armchairs were popular, with deep cushions in the seats, and on short curved legs at the front and splay legs at the back, see plate 20. We were now using English as well as imported walnut, and a taste for less ornate decoration accentuated the importance of good design and careful choice of timber. However, one popular carved motif of the period was the scallop shell which was used to decorate the friezes, front rails, and to cap the knees of the curved legs on all types of furniture. The curved leg in the form it took during the Queen Anne period was the introduction of what we now know as the cabriole leg. Cabriole was a French dancing term meaning a bound or leap, and was therefore used to describe legs on furniture which terminated in a simulated animal's foot below the curved knee. This had developed from the Flemish moulded curve with either the Braganza or animal's foot incorporating the shaped moulded stretcher. During the early part of the eighteenth century the curve of the knee became simplified and often terminated in a simple pad foot, see fig. 33B. The additional strength of this design soon became apparent and the heavy moulded stretcher disappeared.

By this time the interior arrangements of houses had begun to change. The use of large tall windows, imposing fireplaces and doorways required furniture of the same proportions to achieve a balanced effect. Although it was not until the 1720s that this became truly fashionable largely due to the work of William Kent, console or pier tables with tall mirrors over (pier glasses) were already being made. Also, in rooms other than the library, case furniture became taller and narrower.

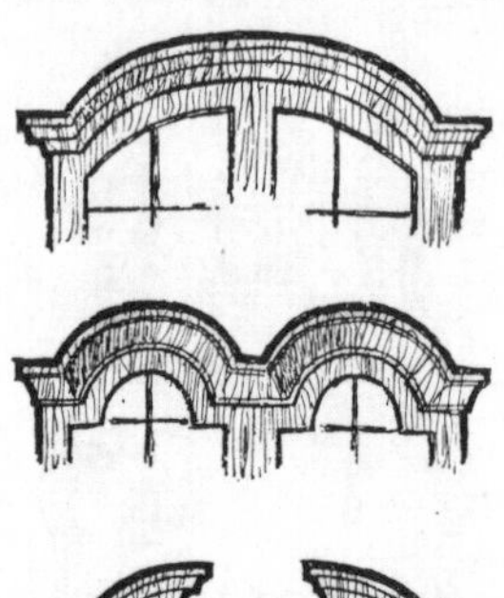

Fig. 35: Three examples of cornice shapes that were fashionable during the first quarter of the eighteenth century.

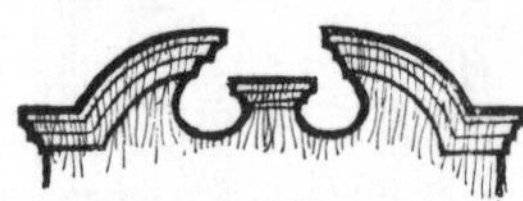

A typical example of this was the development of the bureau-cabinet, of which the earliest types were made in three main parts. The top part of an escritoire, with its deeply sloping front enclosing several small drawers and compartments, was placed on a low chest of drawers base instead of an open stand. Placed on to the horizontal top part of the escritoire was a double door cupboard, having either solid wood or mirror glass panels, which was surmounted by a shaped cornice which at this time would be single, double dome or flat, see plate 22. Some typical cornice shapes are illustrated in fig. 35. In order to make the cupboard 'sit' securely, a substantial moulding was placed around the edge of the escritoire. A similar moulding was placed round the chest/escritoire joint and large metal carrying handles were often fixed on the sides of all three pieces. The feet would be turned bun shape, or later a plain bracket. Some examples of both the bureau and the bureau-cabinet of this period have the base constructed with a row of small drawers placed one above another each side of a recessed compartment which accommodated the knees of the writer. This same construction was used for some types of knee-hole dressing tables and the flat top knee-hole writing desk, see plate 24. The recessed compartment soon disappeared from the bureau, however, for the open lid or 'fall' provided ample space for knees, but the compartment was then difficult to reach. So most walnut period bureaux have three long drawers below a deep top rail sometimes decorated to simulate a drawer front. The space behind this dummy drawer was accessible only by opening the fall which could be locked. Inside, a portion of the top slid back underneath the small drawers and compartments revealing the well. This characteristic disappeared during the 1730s and the space was filled with a proper drawer. Another article which first gained general popularity during the early 1700s was the tallboy. This version of a chest on chest invariably had the bottom drawer arrangement and rail similar to that of the dressing table, with the cabriole legs made suitably shorter, see plate 26.

George I, 1714-1727

George I was born in 1660, created Duke of Cambridge 1706, proclaimed King in 1714, and was crowned at Westminster later that year. He was the first sovereign of the House of Hanover, being the son of the Elector of Hanover and Sophia, grand-daughter of James I. Apart from a Jacobite rising in 1715, and the well-known financial 'South Sea Bubble' the reign of George I was peaceful. Possibly through the lack of personal effect of the King on designs and fashions, coupled with the increased ability of larger sections of the community to afford fashionable houses and furnishings, the leading styles from the early years of George I to about 1800 are generally recognised by the name of the style or its designer instead of the name of the reigning monarch. For example, we refer to Rococo rather than George II; to Hepplewhite or Adam rather than George III, see charts on pages 194 and 195.

From 1710 to 1720 design in general mellowed. A combination of the best features of the previous fifteen years produced a subtle, functional and attractive style of furniture. The outlines formed the basis for many of the elaborate designs of the 1740s and 1750s, and can often be discerned under the extravagant decoration of the Rococo period. The Queen Anne style prevailed well into the 1720s, as if our cabinet makers needed a break to settle down and prepare themselves for the expansive times ahead. The Palladian, Rococo, Gothic Revival and second Chinoiserie styles were to lift some from craftsmen status to high society, making them extremely wealthy in the process. The great age of English furniture had begun.

EARLY GEORGIAN

By the beginning of the eighteenth century, the furniture being made in England can be said to belong to one of three main categories. The first includes the finest pieces, made to the most up-to-date designs by appointed craftsmen for royal and aristocratic households and introducing a new style or a new decorative motif. Second is the furniture made in London and larger towns throughout the country for the moderately wealthy squire and merchant class. This reflected less accurately the introduction of a new style but, because of the sheer quantity made, it laid the foundations for a rapidly expanding furniture industry and forms the bulk of what is today recognised as antique furniture. The third category is the country or cottage furniture made by a retained joiner on a large estate for the houses of the tenants, or by the village carpenter for the cottages of the local people.

By 1720, the craft of furniture making had become a complex industry employing joiners, turners, carvers, gilders, clock and barometer makers, mirror glass makers, fine metal workers and upholsterers. In London and other major cities each branch of the industry became a specialised but integral part in an ever-expanding trade. Construction became the finest in the world, matching even that of furniture made for the French court, and design developed in many ways, with changes influenced by contemporary Europe, by our own historic revivals and by the study of Classical styles. By the 1730s the timber most used for good quality furniture was mahogany and, as had happened with walnut following its introduction, it was used for some time in the solid rather than being cut for veneer. Mahogany lent itself admirably to the skills of a good carver and was a considerable encouragement to the growing taste for the flamboyant Baroque and later Rococo styles, c. 1730 to 1760.

The decade 1720-1730 saw important changes in the design of English furniture and the materials used in its manufacture, but the overlapping of both these aspects occurred to some considerable extent from 1715 to 1745. From the Restoration in 1660 to the later years of Queen Anne, changes in design, methods of decoration and manufacture occurred very quickly. One style ousted another, and affected the countenance of even middle class furniture, quite rapidly. The same cannot be said for the ensuing thirty years. Although mahogany became the standard timber for good quality furniture during the 1730s (see pages 66 and 67) and there was a growing preference for Rococo, the production of walnut furniture did not suddenly cease and furniture of the previous architectural style, particularly wall mirrors and cabinets, continued to be made following the publication of Palladian as well as Rococo and Gothic designs in 1740.

By the 1720s most household articles that we now take for granted were already in use; some of the more notable exceptions are discussed on page 68. It is therefore the difference in style, construction and decoration which make it possible for us to date and authenticate articles of the first half of the eighteenth century, rather than the article itself or its use, which are so often guiding factors in other periods.

The gentle curves of the Queen Anne period continued with little change save slight modification through the reign of George I, but by the late 1720s fashion had changed and furniture of the first quality was made to one of two styles, and completely opposed styles at that—the Baroque and the Palladian (see page 61). The Baroque was by far the more expensive to produce and therefore much more furniture was made in the Palladian manner. Many of the architectural motifs of the latter could be incorporated in middle class furniture and, for a while, Palladian furniture was the height of fashion. But a seed of favour for the unrestrained had been sown by the elaborate Baroque, and from this grew the hybrid Rococo. From the 1730s the Rococo movement developed, greatly encouraged by the publication of the works of the more fashionable designers, the earliest of whom were practising cabinet makers. This is evident when the designs for furniture by William Kent the architect (see page 60) are compared with those of Matthias Lock the maker and carver. Undoubtedly the most quoted of the mid-eighteenth century designers and craftsmen is Thomas Chippendale (see page 63). His *Gentleman and Cabinet-Maker's Director* included fashionable designs for both ordinary and the most elaborate furniture.

The twenty years from 1740 to 1760 were the great age of mahogany furniture, so much of which can be seen to reflect the Georgians themselves and the times in which they lived. The proportions of the furniture are invariably faultless. Mid eighteenth century tables had wide-spread feet in comparison to the size of the top; chairs had good wide seats; tallboys (chest on chest furniture) had tops narrower than bases and bases narrower than feet, and to retain the balance a large overhanging moulding and cornice was placed on the top.

Even the country made pieces have great charm, probably because the designs of the period lent themselves to more simple manufacture without losing their essential character. Unfortunately this observation becomes less true as the century progressed. Country made furniture of the last quarter of the eighteenth century gained little from the severe lines of classicism. The timber employed was usually the cheaper, softer and more open-grained Honduras mahogany or native woods and, while these were much used for veneers and were suitable for curved patterns, strict alignment and straightness was needed for the successful representation of the designs of Hepplewhite, Adam and Sheraton. Because it was basically easier to produce, a vast amount of unattractive but authentic middle class furniture dating from the last part of the eighteenth century is available today, but it lacks a fineness in its proportions and materials.

By the 1750s a considerable vogue for the Gothic and the second Chinese styles had developed. While both of these can be modified for the decoration of English furniture in a most delightful way, their combination with the Rococo can be overpowering. One of the finest examples of both combined and separate second Chinoiserie period decoration is at Claydon House, Buckinghamshire. Here the Chinese Room contrasts strongly with the combined Palladian, Rococo and Chinoiserie decoration on overdoors and frames of alcoves in the adjoining rooms. The Gothic movement was influenced by Horace Walpole and so typified by his house Strawberry Hill that pure Gothic decoration of this period is often referred to as 'Strawberry Hill Gothic'. Many of the motifs, such as cluster column legs, arched brackets and carved battlements, found their way on to more ordinary furniture, but like Chinoiserie, when combined with Rococo much of the essential charm of Gothic was lost.

It would appear inevitable that following the initial introduction of any one extremely popular design, improvement is piled upon improvement until little of the original remains. This was particularly true of the Rococo movement, which by 1760 had run to wild excess and progress now lay through drastic change. This took the form of an overriding passion for the Classical, modified for suitability in all fields of the decorative arts, principally by the architect and designer Robert Adam.

Design and designers, 1720-1760

William Kent (1685-1748) was the first English architect to revolutionise the plan of our houses and design the furniture to go into them. About 1710, during a period of pronounced taste

Fig. 36: The five orders of Classical architecture, from left to right: Doric, Composite, Tuscan, Ionic, Corinthian. Great importance was attached to a detailed knowledge of Classical architecture in general and these orders in particular by designers and craftsmen during the eighteenth century, and variations are shown in design books of the period. Those illustrated in Chippendale's 'Director' are not fluted, but the basic proportions must remain as the original. Apart from the decoration to base, cap and entablature, each has a specified size, e.g. Corinthian and Composite are ten diameters high, Ionic nine diameters high, Doric eight and Tuscan seven.

for Italian architecture, sculpture and paintings, popularised by people returning from the Grand Tour of Europe, William Kent was sent to Italy to study painting. He returned to England in 1719 and thereafter received constant patronage from Richard, third Earl of Burlington. Kent's houses each had a large entrance hall approached from outer steps, and a succession of rooms leading one into another. These great Palladian houses, with their accent on Classical lines, porticoes and the five orders, fig. 36, of which Houghton Hall and Holkham Hall in Norfolk are fine examples, had their interiors designed in the same manner. Door pillars and cornices or 'over-doors', although made of wood, had the lines and proportions of masonry as did much of Kent's furniture, which often lacked the feeling of that designed by a man used to working with wood. His book-cases and cabinets, with columns at the sides and architectural cornices and pediments on top, allowed no consideration of the colours and shading of timber. He did, however, advocate considerable use of part or 'parcel' gilding for the tops and collars of columns and the edges and crestings of cornices, and thereby produced an effect peculiar to this period. Kent also made considerable use of ponderous and ornate Baroque

Fig. 37: An example of a side table in the Baroque taste, c. 1730, in the manner of William Kent. The supporting frame for the marble top would have been decorated with paint, gold or silver leaf, and clearly shows the attempted effect of stone masonry rather than woodwork, a feature strongly apparent in many of Kent's designs.

Fig. 38: A carved console or side table, c. 1745, showing the development from the heavy Baroque to the more gentle Rococo style. It shows a definite French influence and would therefore be more likely to be of pine or lime decorated with paint or metal leaf rather than polished mahogany as on a pure English example.

designs for many large console tables, mirror frames and chairs, fig. 37.

Baroque and Rococo

The word Baroque, applied to furniture, meant any whimsical, idealistic, asymmetrical design of ponderous proportions. Heavy carved scrolls, eagles with spread wings, masks, torsos, amorini, huge sea shells and other fantastic motifs accentuated with gilding and enriched with fine brocades and velvets were the fashion in France and Italy during the last half of the seventeenth century and early eighteenth century, and gained an important but limited popularity in England particularly after Daniel Marot and William Kent. Magnificence without elegance might be a suitable summary.

The word Rococo is derived from the French *rocaille*, meaning freely 'rockwork', and is used to describe in England what was really a refined simplification of Baroque, with rocks, garlands and festoons of floral motifs used for both the background and the highlights of the decoration, see fig. 38. The Rococo style originated in France; Pierre Lepautre, whose work c.1700 gained considerable recognition, Claude Audran (1658-1734), Nicholas Pineau (1684-1754) and later J. A. Meissonnier (1696-1750) were among the leading figures of the Rococo movement. The Rococo style continued in England during the early 1740s

Fig. 39: A design for a torchere or candle stand showing the uncontrolled decoration suggested for fashionable Rococo furniture from 1745 to 1750. This stand would have been polished mahogany or applied with gesso and gilded.

and remained the predominant fashion for nearly twenty years. The two men who pioneered the English version of this French style were Matthias Lock, carver and gilder, and his aide, H. Copland. From 1740 the design books produced by them incorporated asymmetrical and symmetrical carving of all manner of motifs, the C scroll playing a most important part, see fig. 39 and plate 33.

One of the most fashionable cabinet makers, certainly of the second quarter of the eighteenth century, was William Hallett (1707-1781). He was employed by Lord Folkestone, the Earl of Leicester, the Earl of Pembroke and, it is believed, by the Duke of Chandos during the building of Canons, near Edgware, described by Defoe as 'the most magnificent palace in England'. In 1745, the Duke's vast fortune having been dissipated, his successor demolished the house and sold the materials and fittings. Hallett bought the estate and much of the materials and built himself an elegant house on the site of the old one. Hallett's son William predeceased him and his grandson, also William, inherited the estate and Canons. By 1786 the grandson had reached such a social position that his portrait with his wife was painted by Thomas Gainsborough and entitled *The Morning Walk*. Canons is of greatest interest in this text because it was one of the earliest recorded uses in large quantity of the newly imported timber, mahogany, for the construction of the doors and panelling.

Thomas Chippendale: Rococo, Gothic and Chinoiserie

Thomas Chippendale was born in Yorkshire in 1718, the son of a joiner on a country estate. It can be assumed that he was sent to London as an apprentice cabinet maker for little is known of him before 1748, when he married Catherine Redshaw at St. George's Chapel, Hyde Park. He rented large premises including workshops, a timber store and a front shop in St.

Martin's Lane where he entered into partnership first with James Rannie and secondly with Thomas Haig. In 1754 he published the first edition of a book of designs entitled *The Gentleman and Cabinet-Maker's Director*. This contained 160 fine line engravings showing every conceivable type of furniture decorated or formed after the Rococo, Gothic and Chinese tastes. It included many fantastic creations which were probably never produced, but most important, it showed designs for more ordinary household furniture with some of the fashionable motifs as integral parts of the structure. The open fret cut bracket, the 'cluster column' leg, the carved frieze of icicles, or the arch shape open back of a chair are some typical examples. The *Director* was the first publication to be devoted to furniture alone, and the inclusion of designs which could be achieved by the country craftsmen as well as those for the city carver and cabinet-maker made it a great success; the following year a second edition was published. A third and enlarged edition appeared in 1762, being a compilation of a weekly series issued from 1759. However, some of the finest work to come out of Chippendale's own workshop was not made to designs published in the *Director*. By the early 1760s a Classical revival had begun to replace Rococo and it was for the designer and architect Robert Adam that Chippendale produced furniture of outstanding quality and fineness, reviving the use of marquetry to interpret classical motifs in a display of controlled craftsmanship unsurpassed before or since.

Although the practice of Japanning furniture had continued since its introduction to this country during the latter part of the seventeenth century, the taste for Chinoiserie declined during the early part of the eighteenth century. It revived, however, during the early 1740s, being encouraged to a considerable extent by the wide circulation of books on foreign travel. One of the most influential of these was the magnificent work on China by the Frenchman J. B. du Halde, the English version of which was published during 1742 in weekly instalments. Furniture made in the Chinese manner was for the most part carved and the surface decorated with paint, lacquer, or gilding, or left plain to show the beauty of the wood. The frames of mirrors, torcheres, cabinets, bookcases, tables, chairs and all manner of household fittings were constructed with pagoda-shaped tops, figures of Chinamen, long necked birds (called ho-ho birds), blind and open fret cutting in the style of Chinese fencing, fig. 40, and often incorporated some Rococo motifs as well. Therefore mid eighteenth century Chinoiserie can be seen to have become more complex in design and freer in concept than the original.

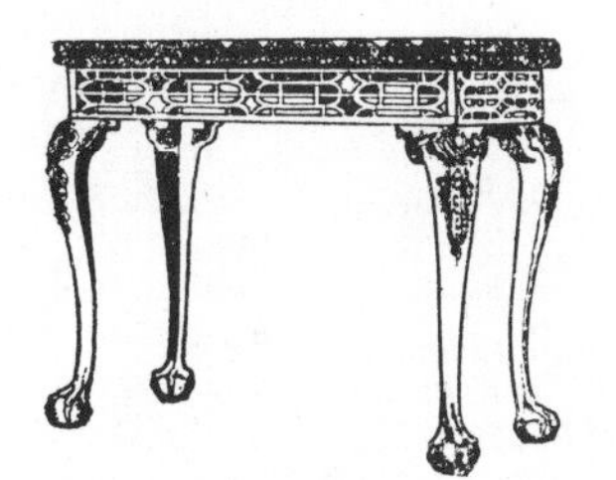

Fig. 40: A mahogany fold-over top card table, c. 1750. This shows the combination of the Rococo and Chinoiserie patterns of decoration. The carving, which stands well proud of the outline of the knees, the cabriole curve, the ball and claw feet, and the carved top edge are made to contrast strongly with the Chinese style blind fret carving on the frieze. Blind fret was produced in two ways during the eighteenth century: the surface is carved in low relief up to a depth of a quarter inch, or is applied with pierced fret cut pieces of wood the same thickness. Through-piercing or open fret was mostly used for chair backs, bookcase pediments and panels in the sides of clock case hoods.

Likewise, eighteenth century Gothic became more eclectic during its most popular period. Gothic taste took as its theme medieval styles, following either a pattern reminiscent of church and cathedral design or of the early castle and its interior. Gothic taste in design had been in evidence since the early 1720s having had only a mild popularity compared to the sweeping Palladianism, but from 1740 to 1765 it reached its eighteenth century height (see Strawberry Hill Gothic, page 60). It would appear to have been a purely English phase, for there are no records of a similar fashion on the Continent, and it is strange that at its greatest popularity, through the romantic designs of Batty Langley, Thomas Chippendale and several other contemporaries, Gothic taste became so fanciful that it bore little if any relationship to its origins. The Gothic style which was revived again during the 1800s showed a much more realistic appreciation of true medieval design, especially in George Smith's *Household Furniture*, published in 1808 (see page 88).

However, mid eighteenth century Gothic is important in this text for like all the preceding designs, it left us with several peculiar motifs which found their way into the furniture of the time. The legs of pot stands, night cupboards (commodes), tables and chairs, etc., might be formed as 'cluster columns', fig. 41. Open fret-cut corner brackets and chair backs had simulated church window shapes as their basis and the cornices and friezes of cabinets were often embattled.

Walnut and mahogany

Walnut had become the most popular timber for the construction and, later, the decoration of good quality English furniture

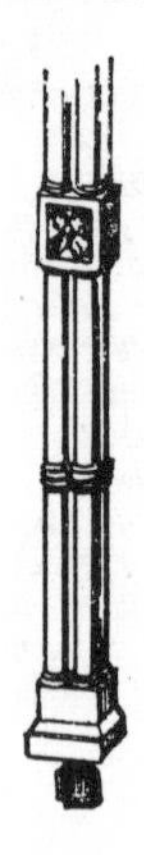

Fig. 41: A cluster column leg, one of the most popular design motifs for English furniture made in the Gothic taste c. 1740-1760.

during the last forty years of the seventeenth century. To supplement the insufficient supply of English walnut we had come to rely on European walnut, considered to be of superior quality and imported mainly from France. Unfortunately a very hard winter in 1709 killed much of the continental walnut and in 1720 its export from France was banned. However, by this time we were also importing walnut from Virginia in North America. Virginian walnut is more like mahogany than English and European walnut, having a straighter grain and often attaining a greyish colour which at first glance appears similar to a faded mahogany. It does not however have the depth of colour or the more attractive markings of the other timbers, and was used more in the solid than for veneer. References made to mahogany in the furnishing of Canons, contemporary bills of lading and other manuscripts, and the considerable amount of mahogany furniture extant that dates from 1730-1750 suggest that the changeover from walnut to mahogany was fairly rapid and occurred around 1730. Walnut continued to be used well into the 1750s, but it was no doubt a minority demand.

In 1721, in order to boost the shipbuilding industry, the British Government abolished the heavy import duty on timbers grown in the British colonies in North America and the West Indies. Among these woods was mahogany (genus *Swietenia*) of which the first type imported to this country and used for the construction of furniture came from Jamaica. This 'Jamaica wood', as it was known, had a close grain with attractive markings, a deep reddish colour, and was found to be more durable than walnut. Also the enormous trunks provided wider planks and the timber was less given to warping and shrinking. It was ideally suitable for carving, and when polished (see page 182) showed great depth of colour. Its almost metallic qualities were not confined to strength, for over the years fine examples of early mahogany furniture have attained an appearance closer to bronze than wood (see Patina, page 182). As mahogany became more popular, other sources of supply were discovered, and we began importing it from San Domingo, Puerto Rico and Cuba. As these islands were all Spanish colonies, the wood from them was called Spanish mahogany, although the Cuban timber, which was much used toward the middle of the eighteenth century, is usually catalogued separately, for it provided more varied grain markings while retaining the other important properties of the earlier Spanish woods. Towards the latter part of the eighteenth century we were importing vast quantities of mahogany from Honduras, but this is easily distinguished from the Jamaican, Spanish and Cuban timber. It is much lighter in weight, has a less attractive appearance and less depth of colour, and has an open grain. It filled the tremendous demand for wood for the middle class furniture produced between 1760 and 1820, but was rarely if ever used as show wood on any fine quality work. By the 1740s mahogany had become the fashionable wood and, like walnut, was used first in the solid and then as veneer. The great age of fine mahogany furniture was the middle of the eighteenth century, with the development of elegant designs by men who knew and loved the timber with which they worked.

One important feature to appear on the curved legs of furniture during the early part of the eighteenth century was the 'ball and claw' foot, fig. 40. This was essentially an Oriental design symbolically portraying the dragon's claw holding the pearl of wisdom. It was used in walnut and then in mahogany furniture until the 1760s, but went out of fashion after the Classical revival. Sometimes the claw of an eagle was used instead of a dragon, and both versions ran concurrently with the pad foot which was already established as a most suitable design for country furniture. The shape of what we term the cabriole leg was actually a double curve which, when reduced in height, made the ogee shape for the bracket feet of chests of drawers, bureau cabinets and bookcases and, during the late 1740s and 1750s, of commodes. By the 1720s it had become the general practice to form the feet of such furniture with a straight sided bracket with some shaping to each end, fig. 42b, a practice which continued until very nearly the end of the eighteenth century. After the 1730s and usually on better quality furniture, the ogee bracket, fig. 42a, became more popular and remained so until the 1770s.

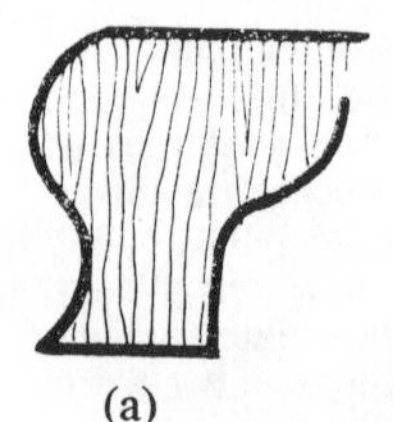

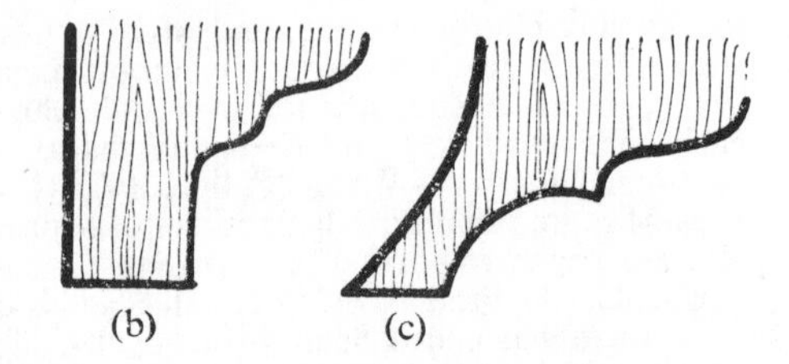

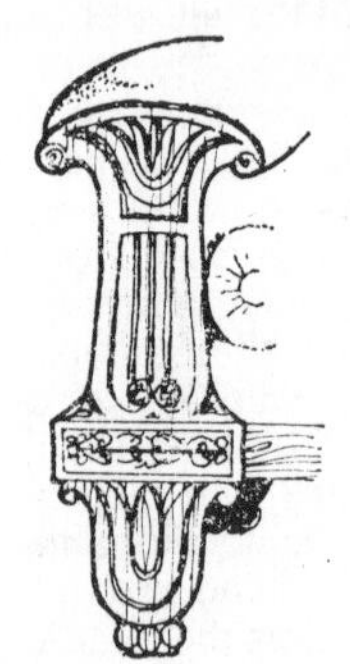

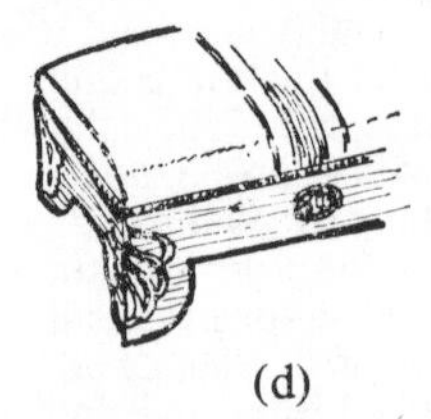

Fig. 42: (a) The ogee bracket foot, popular for fine quality chest and cabinet furniture from c. 1740-1775. (b) The plain bracket foot, most used on more ordinary household furniture from c. 1720-1780. (c) The splay bracket foot, used for fashionable chest and cabinet furniture from c. 1780 to 1810. (d) A Regency bracket foot in the manner of Thomas Hope, shown here with the applied anthemion or formal honeysuckle motif. c. 1805-1825. (e) A late Regency seat end and foot, showing stylised foliate low relief carving. A similar shaped foot was also produced with a turned 'bun' during this period, c. 1820-1835.

Washing stands and night tables

In 1724 Messrs. Gumley and Moore recorded making three tables of mahogany, one 'supping' and the other two 'desart'. This is not only one of the earliest references to mahogany in the manufacture of furniture but it also gives an indication of the now numerous and diverse uses for which articles of furniture were being made. During the 1740s and 1750s several items of furniture first began to appear in quantity. Two such pieces were washing stands and night tables which by the 1760s had become standard equipment for the bedrooms of every well-appointed house. The earliest types of washing stands are sometimes called wig stands, fig. 43, and night tables are referred to as pot-cupboards, fig. 44, or, the larger type, commodes, fig. 45.

The manufacture and use of soap had been known in this

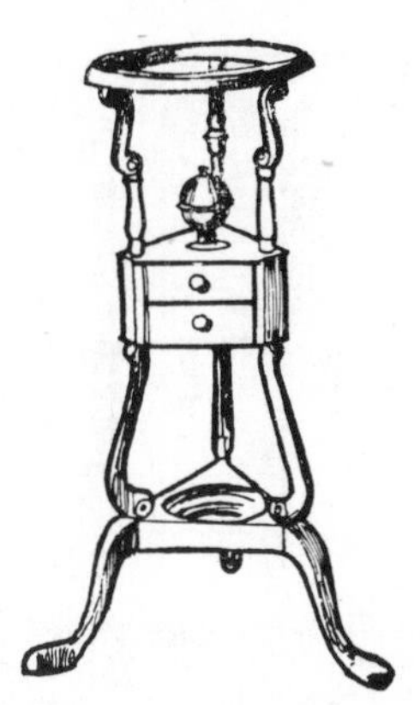

Fig. 43: A tripod base washing stand, often referred to as a wig stand, c. 1750. The top ring held the basin, the lower platform the ewer and above the drawers the spherical cup held the soap which was made in round lumps and known as a wash ball.

country since the fourteenth century, but it was not until the latter half of the seventeenth century that a full cleansing toilet became part of a daily routine, and even then only for a minority

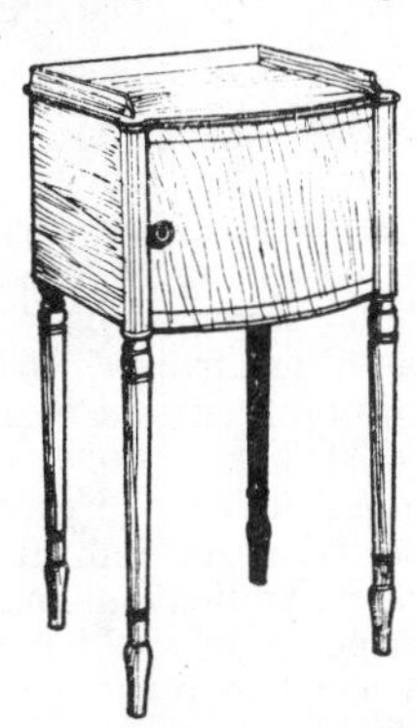

Fig. 44: A mahogany night table or pot-cupboard c. 1800. This type of table was most popular toward the end of the eighteenth century and like the wash stand, fig. 47, was often made to fit into a corner.

Fig. 45: An English night table commode, c. 1770. The front two legs are divided and the drawer pulls out, supported at the back by the runners, to form a seat. Towards the end of the eighteenth century the top doors were often replaced with a tambour shutter. This is a series of thin strips of wood glued to canvas which can be pushed back into the sides of the cupboard compartment.

Fig. 46: A wash stand of the enclosed type c. 1780. Popular from 1760 this type of stand followed to some degree the fashionable decoration of the periods and can often thereby be dated with fair accuracy.

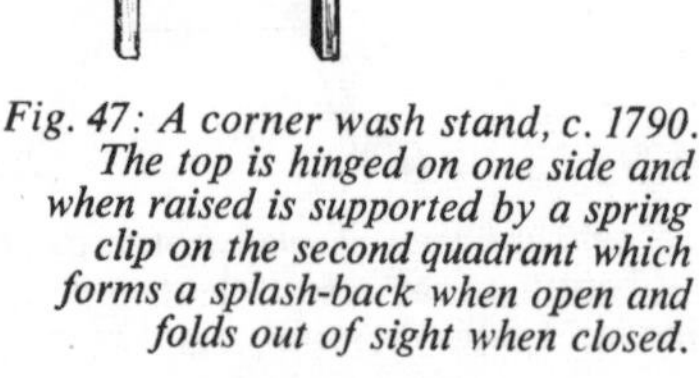

Fig. 47: A corner wash stand, c. 1790. The top is hinged on one side and when raised is supported by a spring clip on the second quadrant which forms a splash-back when open and folds out of sight when closed.

of the population. The introduction during this period of brushes for cleaning teeth and the beginning of an interest in personal cleanliness and appearance suggests that the small occasional table in the bedroom would have had its single drawer full of washing requisites as well as cosmetic preparations (see under William and Mary, page 52). In addition, from c. 1685 until the early part of the nineteenth century, it was fashionable for gentlemen to shave, and from 1720 it was proper to wear a powdered wig. Thus social behaviour added two more reasons for further development in the furniture industry. Despite the earlier demand there are to date no known authentic examples of stands or tables made specifically to hold jugs and washing bowls prior to the 1740s when two main types were being made. One has a folding top which encloses the bowl and soap compartments, fig. 46; the other is of triform shape and quite open. It has a circular ring for the bowl supported by three generally curved uprights above one or two triangular shape drawers; these were on three similar supports terminating on a triangular platform which was usually turned or dished to accommodate a pitcher or small bowl, fig. 47, and the whole thing was raised from the floor by three curved legs. As the soap was produced in round lumps, and was known as a 'wash ball', a small turned spherical cup and cover was often fixed in the centre of the platform above the drawer(s) as the soap box. When this was made detachable, a hole was bored in the base of the cup which then fitted on to a peg fixed to the platform. This type of stand is commonly known today as a wig stand, the theory being that the wig was put on its block, placed in the bowl and then powdered; when not in use the block stood on the bottom platform.

During the second quarter of the eighteenth century the pot-cupboard, night table, and commodious armchair were introduced as a development from the close stool. This type of enclosed chamber pot and seat had been used in large houses and castles since the latter part of the fifteenth century, and during the seventeenth century had become disguised as small trunks and chests. During the first half of the eighteenth century they were usually in the shape of a lift top box with side carrying handles and on four plain bracket feet, either of walnut or later mahogany. Toward the middle of the century close stools were of two main types. One was a small cupboard supported on four tall legs, the other was a larger cupboard with a deep drawer below, of which the front two legs were split and the drawer housing the chamber pot could be pulled out to provide a seat. The commode chair was a large, open frame chair with a loose upholstered seat frame covering the pot which was concealed from the front and sides by a deep shaped rail. One reason that for many years night tables have been referred to in England as commodes was that most of the finest examples of the later eighteenth century were made to look like small chests or cupboards for which the French name was *commode*. This word essentially describes a low chest with drawers, which unlike the English type of chest of drawers is wider in relation to its height, and, being made only for the finer houses, was always the object of the most elaborate or fashionable decoration. After the middle of the century the serpentine and bombe shapes, fig. 48, were much used for the construction of commodes in the French taste, and two doors often replaced the drawers to form a cupboard. The highest degree of skill and accuracy was needed to make a commode and those that can be seen in museums and country houses today afford us a close look at the work of many of the leading cabinet makers and designers of the eighteenth century. When describing a fine eighteenth century chest as a commode, stress or accent is on the first syllable—*com*mode; an English night table has the stress on the last syllable—com*mode*.

Chest furniture

From the 1740s the basic concept of chest furniture did not change. The tallboy with a chest of two short and three long drawers on a high cabriole leg stand was being replaced by the

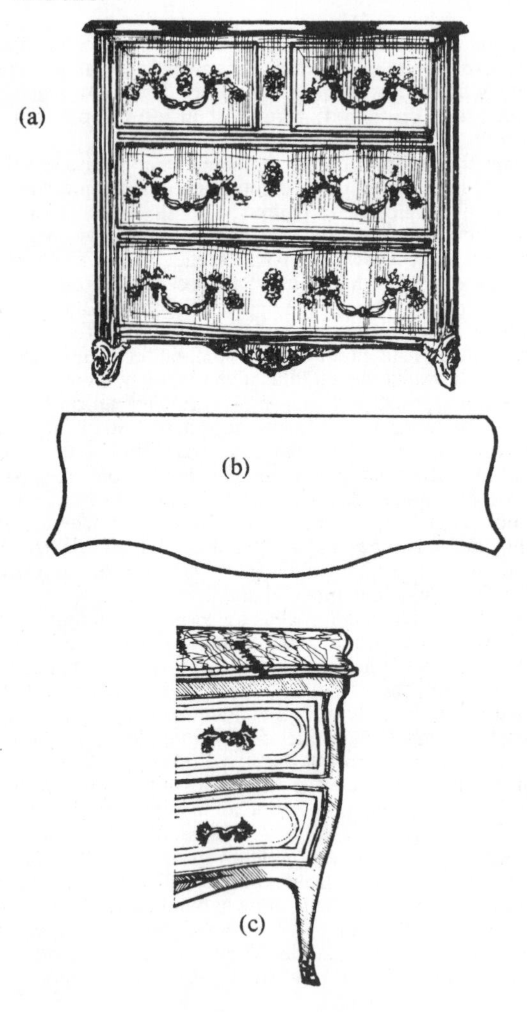

Fig. 48: (a) A mahogany serpentine-shape front chest c. 1755. Strong French influence is apparent in the construction and proportions of this chest, and so it might well be described as a 'commode'. Also shown is the serpentine shape in plan (b) which when used three-dimensionally is called 'bombe' (c).

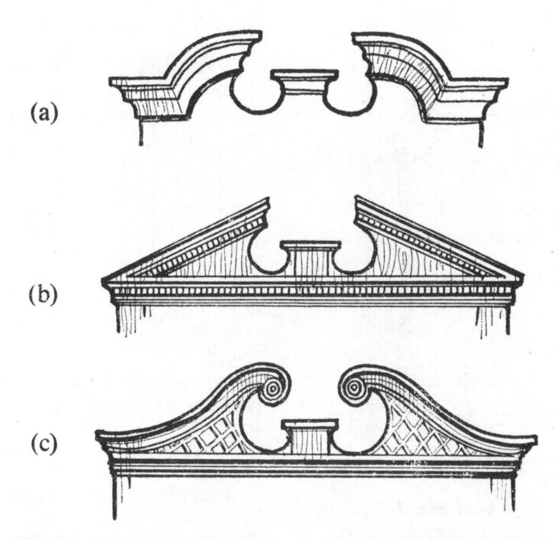

Fig. 49: The development of bookcase and cabinet cornices.
(a) 1700-1730. (b) 1725-1770, the architectural broken pediment.
(c) 1765-1790, the swan-neck cornice shown here with open fret carving in the recessed panels. This type was popular for the crestings of fine mirrors as early as c. 1730.

mid 1730s by one with the base part made of another chest of usually four long drawers on ogee or plain bracket feet and the top cresting became flat, plate 34. The bureau-bookcases and cabinets, plate 22, with either blind (solid wood) or glazed doors to the upper half had similar feet but the top cresting remained an important feature on those of better quality until the 1790s. As a general guide—not to be taken as a definite rule—until c. 1750 these crestings were architectural and most later ones became deeply curved in what is known as a swan-neck cornice and often incorporated pierced fret cutting in the recessed panels, fig. 49. This type had been used for mirror frame crestings since c. 1730. The blind doors were panelled and framed either in straight rectangular form or shaped, the latter being described as fielded panel, fig. 50. The glazed doors progressed quite quickly from plain rectangular frames of six, eight or ten panes of glass with substantial moulding, to a much finer tracery effect with delicate 'astragal' mouldings separating the glass, fig. 51. From 1760 on, glazed doors for furniture attained an unsurpassed quality of design and construction, and as such could be made in the Chinoiserie, Gothic and Classical patterns as

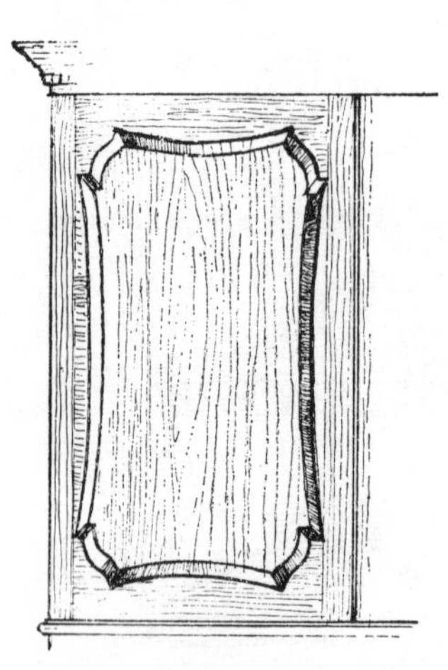

Fig. 50: A fielded panel. Various outlines incorporating this chamfered edge were used to decorate blind doors on cabinets and wardrobes from c. 1730-1770.

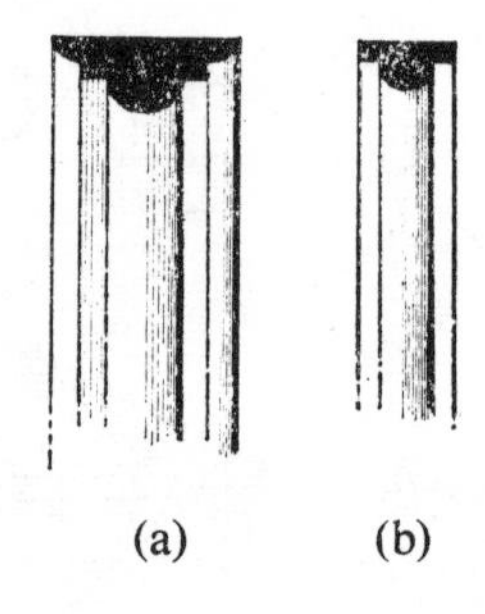

Fig. 51: Astragal mouldings. Used correctly the term astragal describes a semi-circular moulding or bead in architecture, but it has for many years been applied to the glazing bars on English cabinet furniture. The types shown are (a) first half of the eighteenth century, becoming finer as in (b) second half of the eighteenth century.

well as the more usual geometric type, figs. 52 and 53. Of the latter, those having thirteen or fifteen separate panes of glass in each door are regarded as being of better quality. One significant change during the 1730s in the appearance of chest furniture was the shape of the drawer fronts. Following the practice during the early walnut period of placing a single reeded moulding on to the carcase of the chest round the drawer opening, the moulding disappeared, and the drawer front was made to overhang approximately a quarter of an inch all round the drawer. This was formed with a fractional step and a quarter circle section, fig. 54. In many cases the overhang was on the bottom and side edges only, a simulated moulding being worked on to the top edge, thus giving the appearance of shallower drawers and dispensing with the nuisance of the top lip which could snag or catch when the drawer was used. This method of drawer construction continued well into the 1730s and was therefore used on mahogany and Virginian walnut chests of the period. However, by this time a new construction had been introduced, the application of a 'cock bead'. The earliest known examples of this date from c. 1730; therefore it can be safely assumed that a piece with cock beaded drawer fronts will have

Fig. 52: A break-front glazed door bookcase of the type which became popular after c. 1740. By this date such cabinets were made in three parts, the end wings being generally set back to give the break-front effect. The illustration shows a flat moulded cornice, Gothic tracery formed by astragal framework to the glazed doors, and a plain plinth base, c. 1760.

Fig. 53: A mahogany cabinet on chest, c. 1750. The date is confirmed by the rectangular pattern of the substantial glazing bars or astragals and the formal architectural pediment, coupled with the fine quality construction of the chest of drawers base.

Fig. 54: The moulding of the overhanging drawer front which became worked into the top edge of the drawer front prior to c. 1735 when the cock-bead became more popular.

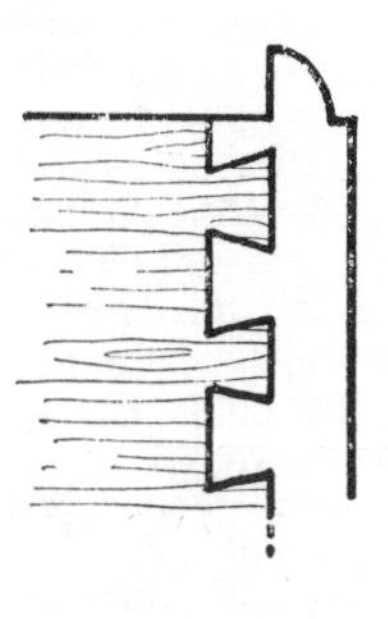

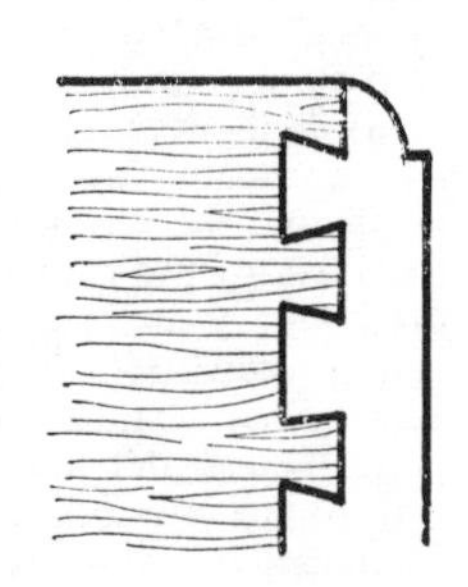

been made after 1735, allowing a few years for the idea to spread and be accepted as an improvement. As can be seen in plate 65 the drawer front is now flush with the carcase and recedes fully into the opening. It is marked however by a thin semi-circular moulding which protrudes up to one eighth of an inch all round the drawer. This can best be described as the extended edge of a frame of veneer, and its application formed the final phase of the construction of the drawer. It proved to be completely satisfactory, for the cock bead remained the standard finish for drawers of good quality furniture throughout the remainder of the eighteenth century. A poor substitute often found on cheaper articles is a line simply gouged out to simulate a cock bead but this is easily discernible and is the mark of, at best, a country made piece.

Dining tables

By the beginning of the eighteenth century it had become fashionable to have a separate room in which to eat. This had occurred during the Restoration period and was encouraged by the plans for houses in the Palladian style by William Kent. It seems strange therefore that little importance seems to have been attached to the designs of dining tables until the second half of the century. There are to date few known published designs specifically for dining tables before 1750, and authentic examples of this period strongly reflect this apparent lack of interest. They are essentially functional in proportion and appearance being relatively undecorated in comparison with other household furniture of the time, and in design follow a natural progression from the gate-leg table which remained popular until the early 1720s. By the 1730s the gate framework had disappeared on fashionable dining tables, and the folding leaves were supported by legs which swung out from a knuckle joint secured to the underframe of the table. At the top the legs were either round in section or square with a caddy moulding on one corner to the depth of the frame. From there the leg was plain round, tapering to a pad foot. On finer examples the cabriole leg was used and this too terminated in either a pad or ball and claw foot, fig. 55. With the latter a carved shell, lion mask or other contemporary motif might be introduced on to the knee of the cabriole, but this is rare and the mark of high quality. The most common type found today is the oval top, club or pad foot, drop-leaf table which can date from 1735 to 1760. The next development was to make the leaves of the table rectangular and add an extra free-standing table to each end to accommodate more people. The ends were generally D shaped or semicircular, and when not joined to the centre

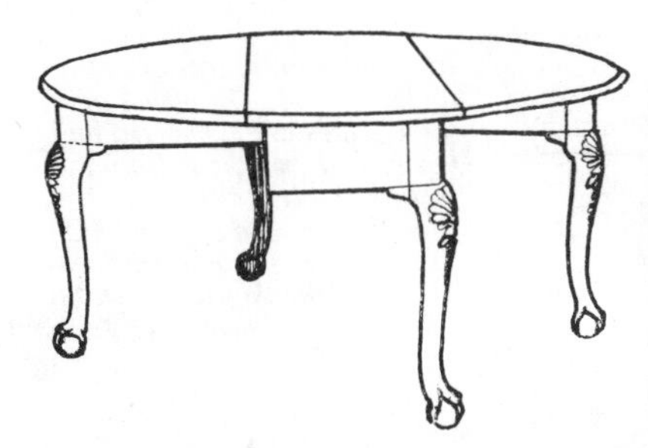

Fig. 55: A drop-leaf dining table c. 1740. The form of folding top and swing-out supporting legs had developed from the gate-leg table and was superseded as a dining table by the centre pedestal type during the middle of the eighteenth century. The drop-leaf table of this period is more often found today with a plain cabriole or turned and tapering leg ending in a pad foot.

part could be used as side or pier tables. It can only be surmised that sometime during the 1740s the legs spaced at intervals around the edge of the table annoyed someone so much that he ordered a dining table constructed in the same way as the then popular tripod base china or tea table, but with four spreading legs instead of three, for by 1750 it is known that dining tables with several centre pedestals were produced. As the century progressed, the shape of these centre pedestals and the splay legs followed the fashionable designs of the period, but strangely the drop-leaf centre with additional D ends and turned legs returned to favour during the early years of the nineteenth century. The centre column table continued to be made, for by this time smaller oval and rectangular tables which we now call breakfast tables were becoming popular. This type of table was a small version of the dining table and could be used for less formal occasions in other rooms.

Breakfast and tripod tables

The term breakfast table correctly describes a table suitable for one or two people at which full breakfast could be served. Considerable importance has been attached to this meal since the fifteenth century, and by the middle of the eighteenth century the most popular type of breakfast table had a rectangular top, a leg at each corner and two shallow drop leaves supported when open by two or four lopers which folded out from the underframe. A stretcher platform was built two-thirds of the way down the legs, and the sides and one end of the table were encased by grills of wire or wood fretwork. The open end was fitted with two doors which were often recessed to give knee room and the compartment was used to contain the china or silver ware. A drawer incorporated in the underframe immediately

Fig. 56: A breakfast or china table, c. 1750. The leaves of these tables are supported on lopers that swing out from the frame; the legs do not move. The drawer held napery and the compartment encased with wire or fret work, shown here in the Chinese taste, held silver or china utensils.

Fig. 57: A pembroke table with serpentine-shape top, fluted frieze and turned and fluted legs, c. 1775. The supporting lopers which swing out from the frame are shown.

below the top held the napery, fig. 56. Most small tables without the enclosed compartment but with the drawer and shallow drop leaves are known as pembroke tables and first appeared during the middle of the eighteenth century. They remained popular for the following fifty years and reliably reflected the changes in style and decoration, fig. 57.

The curved leg terminating in a ball and claw or a pad foot, which for the major part of the first sixty years of the eighteenth century had been the most popular design for both town and provincial furniture, was displaced in favour of straight untapering legs of square section, sometimes with the inside corner chamfered, fig. 58, for those designs following the Gothic and Chinese tastes. It disappeared completely on fashionable furniture with the Classical revival during the 1760s, to return shortly after in a modified version of a French influence commonly attributed to George Hepplewhite. But while chair and most table legs changed quickly from curved to straight (being easier

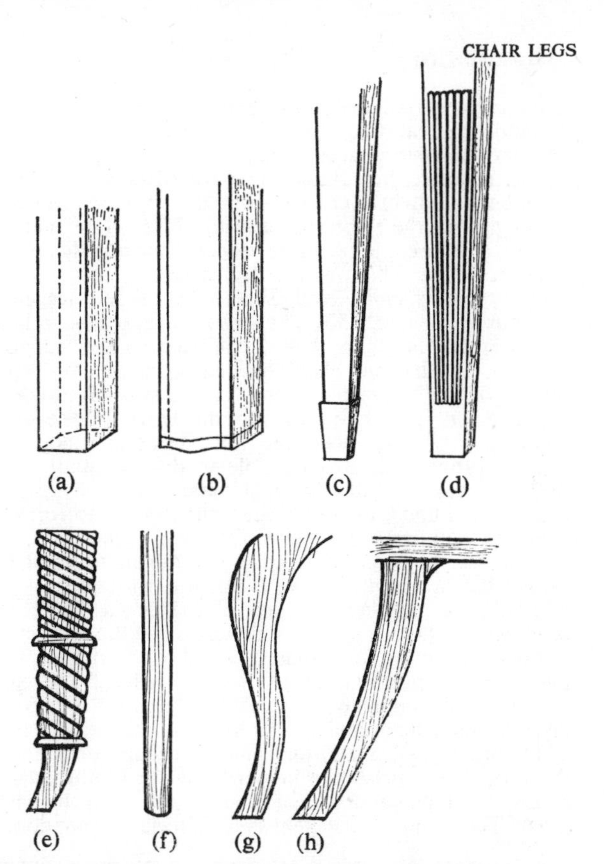

Fig. 58: The development of chair legs from 1750 to 1820. (a) The straight untapered leg with the inside corner chamfered. Often the ground for blind fret work in the Chinese or Gothic manner, or left plain for country furniture, 1750-1765. (b) The straight moulded front leg 1760-1780 which retained the moulding and became tapered c. 1770-1790. (c) The plain taper leg terminating in spade foot, from c. 1775. By 1800 the spade foot had become less popular and the taper leg was decorated with cross-banding and/or stringing. During the early Regency period reeding (d) became popular and is considered more typical of the period than fluting although both were used. Reeding is convex, fluting is concave. (e) Fine and heavy spiral turning and a circular section splay foot, early 1800s. (f) and (g) The return of the elongated ogee curved leg with semi-circular moulding to the front, and straight sides, first quarter of the nineteenth century. (h) The Grecian curved or sabre leg, first quarter of the nineteenth century.

and cheaper to make) one article through its very nature did not abandon the cabriole-type curved leg until much later in the century—the tripod table. The table shown in plate 28 is typical of the turned centre column, three legged table that must surely have been used in every house in the country throughout the larger part of the eighteenth century. Like all definitely shaped articles of household furniture, it had a fine quality and fashionable prototype. This was the dished or tray top china, tea, or supper table which generally superseded the four legged, oblong type during the late 1730s. The tops were dished (slightly sunken) with a raised edge, or had an applied gallery supported by spindles. The baluster shape turning of the column follows the outline of the baluster supports for the stairways and galleries of Palladian houses and is also the basis for the designs of contemporary coffee pots, hot water jugs and tankards. As the century progressed, it is possible to discern small changes in the basic design of this type of table. The baluster shortened into a ball knob which was later 'cut in half' to form perhaps the most popular of all stems, the spiral turned cup, plates 28 and 29. The carving on the knees and the inclusion of the open carved Rococo motive make it possible to date this tripod as c. 1745. The 'gun-barrel' stem of the centre kettle stand in plate 30 had been a standard pattern since the late seventeenth century but was not generally used on more sophisticated mahogany furniture until the second half of the eighteenth century. The combination of this feature with the curved tripod base suggests the stand is therefore country made, not being of the finest quality, c. 1740. The candle stand on the left in the same plate 30 shows the influence of the Gothic taste in the reverse curve legs and some geometric carving at the base of the pillar. The stand on the right is a Victorian simulation.

A Chippendale period tripod table of finest quality had considerable carving on the base and a dished top with probably a shaped rim similar to the border of a good 1750 period silver salver. In fact, the effect was intended to simulate a tray on a stand which, being pivoted on the block under the top, could be tilted upright to stand against the wall when not in use. The vast majority of tripod tables made in the provinces were of course quite plain and genuine eighteenth century dished top tripod tables are rare. But during the early 1900s, furniture of this period was extremely popular and a great many plain tripod tables entered the workshops of skilled fakers to reappear carved and dished (see Fakes and Alterations, page 180). The 'birdcage' top illustrated in plate 29 enabled the table to revolve as well as tip up but although it is accepted as a mark of quality a table without a 'birdcage' is not necessarily inferior.

Fig. 59: The sideboard incorporating drawer and cupboard compartments developed from the serving table and pedestals c. 1780. The latter continued to be made for the finer houses, and by the later Regency period, sideboards with built-in pedestal ends (plate 54) rather than tall legs became popular.

Dining room furniture

Prior to the middle of the eighteenth century the average dining room contained virtually no cupboard space, the napery being brought in by the servants, the cutlery contained in knife cases, and the plate remaining on show on one of the side 'board' tables. In the larger houses these followed the pattern of the other side, pier or console tables in the room and often had a marble top. For the more average household any suitable table was used. By the 1760s however, serving tables with urns on plate warmer cupboards at each end were introduced, and by the 1780s these were incorporated into one piece of furniture, the sideboard, fig. 59. This development coincided with the introduction of a host of items such as plate carriers, dumb-waiters, wine coolers, cheese coasters, bottle sliders and cellarets.

A dumb-waiter is a two, three or four tier stand on a tripod, plate 31. The tiers were formed of circular revolving trays graduated in size and supported on a central column. As the name suggests, dumb-waiters were introduced to stand in the dining room to hold additional foods and cutlery for later during the meal when the conversation might become indiscreet and the servants had been dismissed. The best examples follow the contemporary designs of decoration from the 1740s onwards, for although they are mentioned before, dumb-waiters were not generally popular until after that date. Good quality examples have the trays dished, and a thin unwarped tray shows the maker's careful choice of fine timber. From the lower tray up, each column should unscrew, making the replacement of a broken tray a simple operation. The quality and colour of the timber will usually show if this has occurred recently. During the latter part of the eighteenth century and particularly during the Regency period the bases of dumb-waiters often incorporated complicated sections with drawers and compartments and followed the classical and later heavier styles.

There is often some confusion between a dumb-waiter and a what-not, plate 58, probably because during the later nineteenth century the designs for both were frequently similar. What-not describes a set of usually rectangular trays one above another with the supports at the outer edges and often incorporating one or two drawers in the base. Following its introduction during the last fifteen years of the eighteenth century the what-not was made in various sizes and to all manner of designs.

Still more confusion has arisen regarding the definitions of wine coolers and cellarets. Both these pieces were made to hold bottles of wine and the confusion may well have occurred because during the latter part of the eighteenth century the cellaret was often constructed to serve as both holder and cooler. The earliest known wooden wine coolers or cisterns are c. 1730 and are formed as long open basins lined with lead. They contained ice or very cold water and held the bottles of wine to be served during a meal. After c. 1750 the most popular type was constructed in the same way as a barrel, the sides being straight and sometimes tapering, shaped oval or round and hooped with bands of brass. A tap was inserted at the base and the whole thing was made either to fit into a four-legged stand or to rest on a sideboard pedestal. Cellarets are lidded boxes of oval, round, hexagonal, octagonal or square shape. The interiors are divided into compartments to take a certain number of bottles and, being fitted with a lock and key, they were initially intended to hold a small stock of wine in the dining room at all times. Cellarets came into general use during the 1760s, were lead lined, free standing on feet or legs with castors, and were used extensively until the 1780s when a cellaret drawer was first fitted into one end of the sideboard. The larger and more important types of cellaret continued to be made until the mid-Regency period, but more often with a tap in the base and were therefore used as coolers as well as containers. The ice used was natural frozen water gathered from lakes or pools in winter and stored in deep pits.

Canterburys, Davenports, etc.

Small stands for containing specific items were numerous, often being individually commissioned and later gaining general popularity. One example of this is the Canterbury. According to Thomas Sheraton the Canterbury is either an open box-like stand partitioned to take music, or a shaped stand on tall legs to hold plates and cutlery. The latter is generally referred to today as a plate stand, but the original name for both types is supposed to have derived from the Primate who first ordered the manufacture of such pieces. The Davenport writing desk illustrated in plate 46 is another example. This type of desk dates from the last part of the eighteenth century and is first recorded as being made by Messrs. Gillow for a Captain Davenport. Davenports became popular during the Regency period and, following contemporary designs, were made throughout the nineteenth century. The later types lost the sliding top which formed the knee space and were constructed more like school desks, with the sides supported on turned or scroll columns.

Another writing table that became extremely popular at the beginning of the nineteenth century was the sofa table. This is a long version of the pembroke table with the two leaves at the narrow sides of the top hinged to form drop ends, plate 45. The underframe of the top contains two or four shallow drawers and is supported by a pillar at each end with two splay feet terminating in brass cap castors. The original purpose of this type of table was to provide a writing surface which could be drawn over the end of the sofa, fig. 63; therefore the earlier examples have the strengthening rail high off the ground or arched in a suitable manner. Very soon the rail was lowered and, as it was now visible, decorated to match the rest of the table. During the Regency period, sofa tables with a centre column, shaped platform and curved legs became more fashionable and this type, in gradually increasing degrees of heaviness, remained popular until the 1840s.

By the 1760s most middle class houses had a separate withdrawing room, dining room, hall, reception room and, in some cases, a library. Each of these rooms had to be furnished in the best manner possible and a host of smaller occasional furniture appeared. Breakfast, tea, supper, pembroke and ladies' writing tables were made. For the dining room a dining table, set of chairs, dumb-waiter, wine cooler, cellaret, serving table, plate warmer and probably a large leather draught screen were required. The hall contained at least one console table with pier glass over, hall chairs, a pair of torcheres and a large centre table. And the library had a drum top table, library steps, reading chairs, and a pair of celestial and terrestrial globes. Double chairs, settees, night tables, chests of drawers, bureaux with secretaire rather than slope front compartments, hanging shelves, and wall and corner cupboards went to make up the rest of the appointments in the well-furnished house.

GEORGE III (1760-1820)
THE AGE OF CLASSICISM

Robert Adam

The accession in October 1760 of George III, grandson of George II, had little effect on the sweeping change of fashion from Rococo to Classical. Indeed such was George III's preference for the simpler things in life that he soon gained the nickname of 'farmer' George, and it was left to the fashionable architects, designers and manufacturers of the day to produce and advocate any changes in style and taste. Classical designs had been a steady influence on architecture and, to a certain degree, furniture since the 1720s following the influence of William Kent. However, by the early 1760s the work of Robert Adam, who had been completing his architectural education in Rome with the study of antique designs and decorations, began to have a visible effect on current fashion in this country. The baths of Caracalla and Diocletian, Hadrian's villa at Tivoli, the basilicas and vaulted temples at Herculaneum which Adam visited in 1754, were all to affect the work of English craftsmen within the next ten years. Adam's designs were a definite personalised version of the Classical, whereas Kent's adhered much more strictly to the original. It is interesting to note that at the end of the eighteenth century a neo-classical movement occurred (1799-1830) wherein the designs produced deviated hardly at all from the Roman and Italian models. But the basic idea was the same—simplicity and elegance in outline, and the appearance of height and space and the use of geometrically balanced curves and tapering columns. Adam designed houses and their interiors to incorporate such motifs as husks, urns, festoons, anthemion or honeysuckle, and rams' head masks in the door furniture, wall hangings, mantelpieces, overdoors and cornices, as well as in the carpets, furniture, silver, fine cut glass and porcelain. A particular example of the way in which Adam's designs influenced every field of the creative arts is the contemporary work of the potter Josiah Wedgwood.

George Hepplewhite

For furniture Adam decreed various forms of surface decoration which enhanced and accentuated rather than detracted from the essentially simple and elegant outline. Much of the early Classical period furniture shows the use of incised and applied carving on plain mahogany, but by 1770 veneer work had again become popular and so too had its natural partner marquetry. Some of the finest marquetry of this period was executed to designs of Robert Adam by Thomas Chippendale and John Haig, plate 42. Furniture made strictly to Adam's designs was intended only to go into the great country and London houses where he or his contemporary followers were employed at the time. And just as the Rococo, Gothic and Chinoiserie styles had been presented to furniture makers throughout the country by Thomas Chippendale, so the designs of Adam were spread to a far wider field by the work of George Hepplewhite. Comparatively little is known of this man, and it is largely because of the three hundred illustrations published in his *Cabinet Maker and Upholsterers' Guide* in 1788, two years after his death, that his name is so well known. That he had practical knowledge of a workshop is substantiated by the fact that he was at one time an apprentice to the firm of Gillow of Lancaster and by 1760 had established a shop in Cripplegate in London. The *Guide* was actually published by Hepplewhite's widow Alice, and was such a success that a second edition was published in 1789 and a third in 1794. Hepplewhite only incorporated those designs of Adam he thought most suitable for furniture. There appear no military trophies or rams' head masks on Hepplewhite's designs. Excluded too was the use of classical scenes painted in panels forming the focal point on an article. He made use of oval and round paterae (carved and usually applied discs), swags, husks, flower and bell festoons, and fluting, and although he did not invent he certainly popularised the heart and the shield as shapes for chair backs. He almost certainly introduced the use of simulated Prince of Wales feathers as a motif, although the idea might have stemmed from the designs for some chair backs by James Wyatt, a young and successful architect of the period. Running concurrently with this was a strong

Fig. 60: A window seat c. 1780, showing French influence in the curving frame. Small window seats were more popular in England after 1775.

French influence which can be seen in the curving lines of small window seats, fig. 60, and open armchairs of this style between 1770 and 1790. As this was, like most influences, a modified version attributed to a leading designer of the time in this country, it is generally referred to as 'French Hepplewhite'.

Thomas Sheraton

Straight tapering legs, delicacy of framework and general fine proportion in furniture continued and improved until the end of the eighteenth century, reaching its zenith during the 1790s. The designs of Thomas Sheraton in his *Cabinet-Maker and Upholsterer's Drawing Book* (published in three parts from 1791 to 1794) are the best examples of this. Sheraton was born in Stockton-on-Tees in 1751 and is believed to have come to London during the early 1790s. He was trained as a practising cabinet maker but there is to date no proof that he actually made furniture to his own designs. He was an extremely competent draughtsman and author of various works on philosophy and religion. But his *Drawing Book* presents us with the most comprehensive picture available of good quality furniture of the late eighteenth century. It was regarded in the same way by contemporary craftsmen all over England, and for the most part his designs were faithfully reproduced. Thus the majority of good quality furniture of this period is today recognised as being 'Sheraton'.

Sheraton took for his designs points of style and decoration from his predecessors and contemporaries and, blending them in a most delightful way, produced designs of unique elegance in English furniture. After the turn of the century, Sheraton became more affected by the formal Classical movement and in 1803 published the *Cabinet Dictionary*. In this he illustrated the French and Grecian styles, and advocated much use of animal figures, torsos, heads and feet as important features. This affected both fine and more ordinary furniture, a typical example being the plain brass cap type of castor, fig. 65, which became realistically cast to represent a lion's paw. This pattern remained popular until the early 1820s, at which time an acanthus leaf became more fashionable.

The tremendous following that fashionable architects and designers had during this period means that there must have been an unprecedented number of extremely wealthy patrons. This in turn can be related to the economic situation in England which had gone from strength to strength under the Whig administration. The signing of the Treaty of Paris in 1763 had signalled the end of the Seven Years War with France and had opened up new areas for commercial expansion, hence more French influence. The pattern of higher social behaviour also contributed to the vast amount of domestic articles produced to a set design during this period. Great interest in history and the arts in general promoted circles of friends to follow particular lines of study, so various groups covering large areas of the country attained considerable uniformity within themselves.

This can be easily understood when considering the complex social pattern which developed during the last quarter of the eighteenth century, with so many different influences vying for popularity and each gaining sufficient importance to affect in some degree even the more ordinary household article in some particular piece of decoration.

It is possible to imagine by the end of the eighteenth century in England a complex society similar to that of today. There were 'avante-garde' extremists, the more staid aristocracy relatively unconcerned with all but established good taste, the wealthy untitled trying desperately to keep up with both, the middle class managing nicely and the poor, as always, poor and unaffected by fashion. It is therefore difficult to categorise in chronological order the different tastes and fashions that were at some time popular and important to our furniture history from 1799 to 1825, and the brief description which follows is intended to show rather how much was going on during this period than the chronological introduction of any one style.

Henry Holland

By the end of the eighteenth century a movement for pure Classical designs as against the modified versions of Adam had set in, and what is known today as the Neo-classical Movement began. This was partly affected by and partly coincided with the acceptance of some of the designs of furniture made for the avante-garde Prince George. His importance in the world of design and fashion at this date explains why typical furniture of the period from 1800 to 1830 is generally referred to as Regency, although the constitutional Regency was only from 1811 to 1820. Prince George's architect and principal furniture designer from 1783 until 1806 was Henry Holland, whose designs in the Graeco-Roman and Chinese manners were to affect our furniture history for long after his death in 1806.

In 1783, the year of his coming of age, George, Prince of Wales, received Carlton House as his London residence, and Henry Holland was appointed to rebuild and redecorate it. Thus his Graeco-Roman designs were already established well before the end of the century. These were very much influenced by the French taste of the Louis XVI, the Empire and the Directoire periods, for the French Revolution, the Napoleonic Wars and the Bourbon Restoration were important contributing factors in the complex changes of Regency fashion.

Thomas Hope

To enable the flourishing of the decorative arts there have to be patrons. Occasionally a patron does more than supply funds, and himself makes an important contribution to the arts; indulging a life's interest and a fortune in producing ideas for others to follow as well as the patronage to make it possible. Such a man was Thomas Hope, 1770-1831. While his name is often connected with a minor and somewhat eccentric furtherance of the Egyptian taste, the truth is that Hope produced designs for furniture and interior decoration in the purest Egyptian, Grecian and Roman styles. Essentially these were for his house in Duchess Street, London, and later The Deepdene, near Dorking in Surrey. Both were altered to house his collections of classical bronzes, vases and other antiquities, and the furniture and settings were intended to enhance them. However, in order to encourage this taste, Hope published a book of his own drawings —*Household Furniture and Interior Decoration*—in 1807 (see chart on page 195). This showed his outstanding ability as a draughtsman and designer, from complete room schemes to separate pieces of furniture and individual motifs. He incorporated and popularised many motifs of the French Empire period and the use of black and coloured paint with gilding in the manner of the ancient Egyptians. In fact it is only in recent years that Hope's great contribution to design has really been appreciated.

George Smith

While the original in any fashion remains exclusive, certain modifications will generally ensure a wider appeal. The early nineteenth century was the beginning of an age when more people than ever before were in a position to afford the fashionable material comforts of their choice, and the selection available was the most varied ever known. One of the chief exponents of the modified versions of the classic of this period was the cabinet-maker and upholsterer George Smith. His first major work *A Collection of Designs for Household Furniture and Interior Decoration*, published in 1808, set out his ideas and showed a somewhat light-hearted treatment of classical styles. His excessive use of animal figures, the sphinx, griffins, lions and leopards, and the bold use of anthemion (stylized honeysuckle), acanthus and palm leaf motifs can be said to typify the main essence of the Regency. The revival of lacquer, both Chinese and Japanese, of caning for back and seat panels of chairs, and of buhl, and the continuance of part gilding gave the period tremendous variety.

The Chinoiserie taste of the period was considerably more delicate in form than the two previous periods during the late seventeenth and mid eighteenth centuries. Both Chinese and Japanese lacquer work were popular decoration, especially for door panels of cabinets and cupboards. The essential difference between the two is difficult to describe but easy to see. Basically the Chinese work had a free and almost romantic use of human figures often brightly coloured, whereas the Japanese was more formal, with scenes of sparse landscapes depicted in gold, silver and copper colours and relying to a great extent on simplicity for much of its appeal.

Gothic, Trafalgar and Buhl

During the later years of the constitutional Regency there was a marked decline in the demand for the simple, elegant furniture of the early Sheraton type. Design generally became more bulky and decoration more ornate and heavy. By 1820 there was a strong feeling for the Old French and a Gothic revival, which was to last in various forms for the next seventy years, was well established. While nearly all the books of design for household furniture produced since Chippendale's *Director* had shown one or two articles in the Gothic style, it was not until the later Regency that Gothic became again prominent. This coincided with the decline in the use of marine subjects as decoration or for complete pieces in about 1815, see plate 50. The inclusion of such features as dolphins, cables, cannon, anchors and shells began at the time of our great naval victories under the command of Lord Nelson, about 1803. His death in 1805 also affected furniture design; the back splats of chairs were carved to simulate the drapery around the admiral's sarcophagus, and it is from this date that a preference for ebony or blackened stringing (see Veneer, pages 114 and 189) replaced the previously popular light and contrasting variety. Dolphins had been important decorative features on fine furniture of the

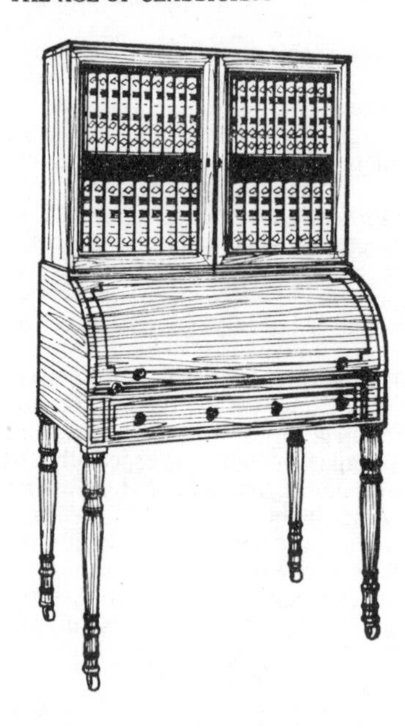

Fig. 61: A mahogany cylinder fall writing desk with bookcase over, c. 1805. The quadrant section lid folded back into the desk and a writing platform could be pulled forward by means of the second row of knobs. Variations of this type of desk were made after the 1790s. The illustration shows one of fine quality timber, decorated with ebonised stringing, finely turned legs and shallow cup castors.

William Kent period, but the early nineteenth century versions were generally of lighter proportions. Ebony stringing, usually on a ground of finely figured mahogany, remained popular until c. 1815 when lines of brass became more fashionable. At about this time a fashion for buhl decoration began and this too, like the Gothic, remained in varying degrees popular for the next seventy years. Buhl work is a type of marquetry using sheet brass and tortoiseshell and was yet another revival from the late seventeenth century and an influence from France. See page 115. The best known Englishman to work both with buhl and brass inlay was George Bullock, a stonemason, upholsterer and cabinet-maker. For distinctive decorative designs Bullock favoured the representation of both naturalistic and stylized English flowers and was keen to use native timbers. Thus pollarded oak and elm became popular for some fashionable furniture during the mid Regency period.

Old French

From 1820, when the Prince Regent became George IV, until 1830, when he died, taste seems to have gravitated towards

Fig. 62: Two late Regency crestings, showing the use of formal foliage portrayed in a free classic manner 1825-1835.

the Old French, particularly that of the Louis XIV period. With the fashion for buhl, large ormolu or gilt metal mounts often surrounding embossed metal plaques depicting classical scenes became popular (ormolu, page 95). These were mostly incorporated on ebonised furniture such as the long, low cabinets and commodes that continued to be made for the next sixty years, although the later almost mass-produced models are of a vastly inferior quality. Also during this time the woods of mahogany and oak became used more in the solid, and in general less furniture was painted although gilding, to emphasise some decorative motif, continued.

The use of classical motifs on the more ponderous furniture of the late Regency gave way to the use of carved, stylized floral motifs on much the same basic shapes. The lotus leaf, which was a popular motif of the period, is a particularly notable example, see fig. 42e on page 68. Designs for furniture and interior decoration of this period are probably best typified and illustrated in George Smith's last publication of 1828, *The*

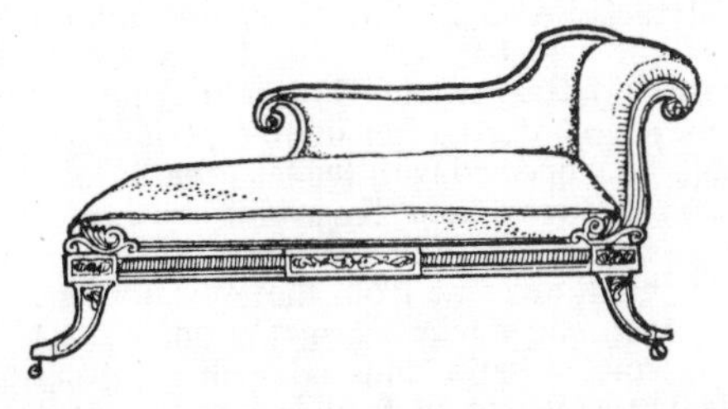

Fig. 63: A Regency period sofa, c. 1810. The terms sofa, couch, day-bed, chaise longue, settle and settee all describe long seat furniture. The first four are generally used today to describe such pieces on which the sitter may recline, whereas settles and settees are seats for more than one person. The word sofa first appeared in this context in England at the beginning of the eighteenth century and chaise longue appeared during the 1790s. The illustration shows the half back single end sofa over which a sofa table might be drawn.

Cabinet Maker's and Upholsterer's Guide. Herein are designs for sofas and sideboards, bed drapes and curtains.

By 1830 the taste for the Old French was under way. In 1827, Crockford's Club had its interior decor redesigned in the Louis XIV style by Phillip and Benjamin Dean Wyatt, and within three years the French taste had become popular for most fashionable bedrooms and boudoirs; while the heavier and more formal 'Modern Greek' was still considered proper for the masculine apartments. It is with these two overriding styles that the complex pattern of the Victorian age began, to change rapidly with the introduction of more and more ancient English and foreign influences in a period of industrial invention and the greatest exhibitions the world had ever seen.

Decoration and materials

During the latter part of the eighteenth century English furniture made in mahogany and in the French taste was usually left undecorated. Any decoration used was either of gilded gesso, i.e. the application of gold leaf on to a previously prepared surface of whiting and size (see description of the process on page 25) or painting with white or pastel colours which could be enhanced with gilt. Pine and lime were found to be more suitable to receive gesso and paint than mahogany, and both woods were much cheaper. This guide does not apply to furniture made in the Classical taste of the same period. Exotic timbers for veneer were further 'improved' with painted panels depicting mythological and classical scenes by such artists as Antonio Zucchi, Angelica Kauffman, and Michele Angelo Pergolesi. Also at this time, fine marquetry of such timbers became widely used, and the cupboard by Messrs. Chippendale and Haig, plate 42, is a magnificent example of classical marquetry decoration of this period. The two woods most popularly connected with the last quarter of the eighteenth century are satinwood and rosewood, but there were many others. The species of satinwood used on the finest quality furniture at this time came from the West Indies. It had a fine golden yellow colour, a hard straight grain, and such depth that it closely resembled satin material with an occasional irregularity. This type came mostly from Puerto Rico and was used for veneering on to mahogany or pine until the end of the century when Sheraton suggested its use in the solid.

A second type of satinwood was imported from the East Indies but this did not come into general use for furniture until the early part of the nineteenth century. It had a more shallow, lemon colour with closer, smaller markings, and it has not as yet matured to the richness of the West Indian variety. This type was used extensively in the solid during the late nineteenth century.

Rosewood came from first the West Indies and later the East Indies and Brazil. Like satinwood it was used for veneer and decoration before being used in the solid. It is generally a dark wood with red-brown streaks accentuated by darker brown or black markings. The covering of protective polish (see page 182) that was applied to most furniture at this time has allowed some rosewood articles to attain a mellow and well figured appearance. If this original polish is removed, however, rosewood tends to turn black and much of its beauty can be lost. Three other types of wood having streaky and contrasting grain are kingwood, tulipwood and zebra wood. They were all used as veneers for panels and bandings rather than in the solid. Kingwood is more like satinwood in general colour appearance, but has greater contrast between the dark and lighter deep golden markings. Tulipwood is sometimes confused with rosewood because its tendency to fade lessens the contrast between the dark and light markings which, when the wood is freshly cut, vary from deep red to yellow. Zebra wood is a hard, close-grained timber with fairly close and very pronounced markings of light yellow and dark brown.

Towards the end of the century, to add contrast in figure as well as colour on a piece of veneered furniture, use was made of curly grained wood and burr cut timbers. In addition to those already known such as the burrs of oak, alder, elm, yew and maple, two new types were used; amboyna wood and thuya wood. Amboyna, with its pleasing light brown colour and 'bird's eye' figuring was used extensively for both complete surfaces and banding and was imported from the West Indies. Thuya was imported from Africa and had similar figuring but a much deeper colour than amboyna. During this period, and even more so during the early years of the nineteenth century, an enormous variety of highly decorative timbers were used. They are generally classified as belonging to one of three main recognisable types; those of essentially uniform colour but with great depth, of which certain cuts of mahogany, satinwood, oak, maple, harewood and ebony are the best examples; those with contrasting streaks in the grain such as rosewood, kingwood, zebra wood, tulipwood and coromandel; and those with the burr of pollarded figuring such as amboyna, alder, oak, elm, maple and thuya.

Metal mounts

By the 1750s a separate yet integral industry connected with the furniture trade had developed; the manufacture of metal

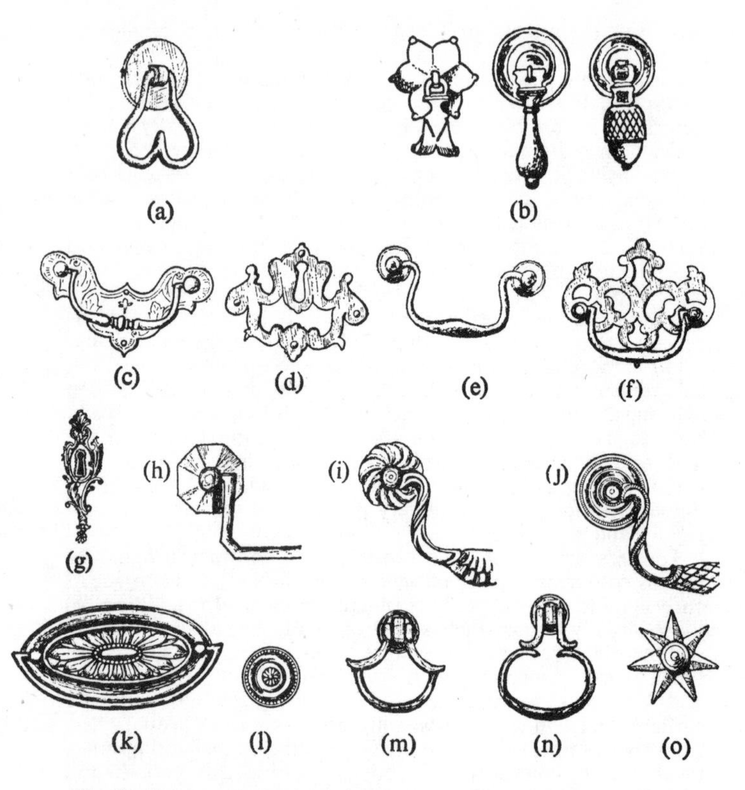

Fig. 64: Some typical handles of the seventeenth, eighteenth and nineteenth centuries.
(a) Iron inverted heart shape drop handle, early seventeenth century. (b) Brass pendant handles, early eighteenth century. (c) Engraved back-plate loop handle of cast brass, early eighteenth century. (d) Pierced escutcheon, later part first half of eighteenth century. (e) Loop or swan-neck handle of cast brass, second half of eighteenth century. (f) Pierced back-plate loop handle, c.1760. (g) Cast brass escutcheon in the Rococo manner, mid eighteenth century. (h) Cast brass loop handle with octagonal rose, French style, second half of the eighteenth century. (i) and (j) Two types of decoratively cast and chased loop handles with roses, later eighteenth century. (k) Stamped sheet brass back-plate loop handle, after c. 1780. (l) Stamped brass knob with screw fixing, late eighteenth century. (m) Cast brass drop handle, c. 1775-1800. (n) Cast brass drop handle, c. 1750-1775. (o) Regency period star knob.

mounts. Iron locks had been used on chests since the fourteenth century. These were the outside plate type, which during the fifteenth century became more decorated. Such advances were made in their manufacture that by the sixteenth and early seventeenth centuries cupboards for downstair rooms had concealed locks with the keyhole protected by a plate escutcheon. Either as part of this plate or fixed separately was a wrought inverted heart shaped handle, which on country oak and fruitwood furniture was used until the early part of the eighteenth century. During the latter part of the seventeenth century, however, the forging of furniture mounts and locksmithing became separate occupations from that of the general blacksmith. The Oriental lacquered furniture that was imported to this country in such vast quantities after the Restoration bore large double plate escutcheons, corner guards and angle straps; naturally, as increasing amounts of imitation lacquered furniture were produced in England the metal mounts had also to be reproduced. For a considerable time the fine quality of the chased decoration on the original eluded the English manufacturers, but the importance of metalwork on furniture had been established and materials other than iron began to be used, and from the latter part of the seventeenth century brass continued to be the most popular. The development of drawer handles and escutcheon plates is shown in fig. 64. Until the latter part of the eighteenth century metal mounts of this type were cast from a mould, 'finished' by the chaser and engraver and then either polished and lacquered or gilded. Although gilt metal mounts of the finest quality were produced in France from the end of the seventeenth century, it was not until the 1760s and after that the equivalent or anywhere near it was produced in England. These were known as ormolu mounts and the word ormolu has since become used to describe any gilt metal mounts on English furniture. By the time the word was used in England during the latter part of the eighteenth century, it was discontinued in France in favour of the term *bronze d'ore*. This accounts for the supposition in England that ormolu applies only to work executed in gilt bronze. This is not necessarily true; ormolu can be any fine gilt metal, for the derivation is from *or moulu*—ground gold; therefore either gilt brass or bronze can be described as ormolu. The main method of applying the gold was mercurial gilding. This is done by mixing gold and mercury to form an amalgam, applying it to the surface of the metal which is then heated to evaporate the mercury and leave the gold firmly fixed. (This method is no longer used as the fumes from evaporating mercury can be lethal.) The development of the metal mount industry in England, and at one time the sale of English ormolu in France, can be attributed to one man—Matthew Boulton (1728-1802). Boulton was the primary figure in the production of fine metalware and from his workshops in Soho, Birmingham, came clocks, silver plated wares, and ormolu. His mounts were incorporated in designs for the finest furniture by the Adam brothers and their contemporaries. During this time the mounting of semi-precious stone to form such delightful articles as cassolets (decorative candlesticks of classical shape, the sconces of which can be reversed to form pot-pourri vases) became popular. Apart from the changes in design of handles and escutcheons during the late eighteenth century and Regency periods the most significant metal mounts on furniture were the castors or small wheels which enabled a piece to be moved easily from one place to another. A simple form of castor was no doubt in use for some special pieces of furniture as early as the sixteenth century, but the full use of such a fitting was apparently not recognised until the end of the seventeenth century. At this time was introduced a wooden wheel on an axle secured to a pin which allowed movement in any direction, and during the early 1700s small hardwood rollers were used on domestic furniture. By the 1740s and 1750s the rollers were made of leather, being several washers placed together on the axle, and the pin was secured with a brass plate which was screwed to the underside of the foot, fig. 65. While ball-and-claw and pad feet provided space enough for this plate the tapering legs and feet of the post-1760 period did not. Therefore a cup-type castor which fitted over the end of the leg was introduced. This, which after c. 1770 was all made of brass, was at first straight and later tapered in shape, and those of the 1775-1800 period often represented the spade feet which were so popular at this time, fig. 65. The cup castor on the horizontal, as in the case of a tripod base, was introduced as an alternative by Thomas Sheraton, and from 1790 to 1830 can give us a good idea of whether or not the fitting is original. The first of this form to appear was basically rectangular with the edges slightly chamfered and followed the end of the line of the leg. An alternative was the same shape with a raised lip. Soon after the turn of the century, a realistically cast lion's paw was the most popular type of castor, but by 1820 this too had gone out of fashion to be replaced by the formal leaf and other typical design motifs of the period, see fig. 65.

Veneer and marquetry

Veneer is a thin slice of wood applied to the basic structure of a piece of furniture as a form of decoration. It was first used in England during the Restoration period, c. 1670, and was origin-

34. (Below) A mahogany tallboy, c. 1770. The upper half is surmounted with a wide overhanging moulded 'dental' cornice and has canted (chamfered and fluted) corners. The base has a pull-out brushing slide over three drawers and bold ogee bracket feet. The handles and escutcheons are original. Note that the retaining moulding is on the base as it should be.

35. (Above) A fine early Georgian Virginia walnut dining chair, c. 1730, showing the still present Dutch influence in the hooped back, compared to the swept-up back rail of the slightly later Rococo fashion shown on the chair in plate 37. The good-shaped cabriole leg has original carving and terminates in a pad foot.

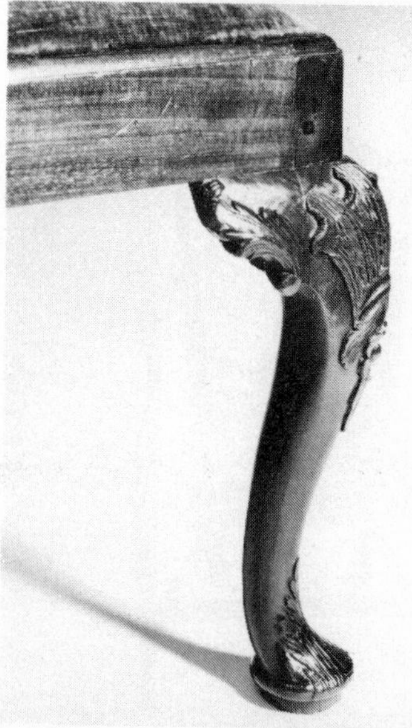

36. (Right) A detail of a leg of the chair illustrated in plate 35, showing the original carving to the knee and pad foot standing well proud of the line of the curve. Also clearly evident and a good thing to see is the end of the tenon peg.

37. (Left) A mahogany dining chair, c. 1750. The pierced back splat, shaped top rail and arm supports have carved foliate decoration in the Rococo manner, and the cabriole front legs terminating in bold ball and claw feet continue this theme in the decoration on the knees. All carving can be seen to stand proud of the outline of its curve. The close nailed upholstery finishes above a gadroon edge (spirally lobed), a motif also popular for fine contemporary silverware.

38. (Right) A mahogany dining chair, c. 1760. The pierced back splat shows an increased formality in its design, yet retains small Rococo features and includes blind fret lozenges. The fact that the straight untapered legs and the simple arms are left undecorated suggests a country made chair. However, it is not uncommon to find one extremely fine portion in an otherwise plain article of this period.

39. (Left) A mahogany dining chair, c. 1775. This chair clearly shows the development from plates 37 and 38 in the influence of the Classical movement. The serpentine-shape top and lower rails of the back, the graceful pierced splat and the square tapering legs are the important features. The drop-in seat had become popular by 1760.

40. (Right) A shield-back chair which typifies the ideas behind fashionable design of the later Classical period of Robert Adam's influence. The vase-shaped back, tapering legs and most delicate structure throughout might be painted with floral motifs as in this case, ebonised and lined or left plain satinwood and polished (c. 1790).

41. (Left) A Hepplewhite period mahogany reading chair, commonly known as the 'Hogarth' style. A deeply moulded arm and leg section is typical of this period, c. 1775, and this type of chair was most popular in gentlemen's clubs and libraries during the latter part of the 18th century. The front section of the left arm has a socket into which a reading stand could be fitted.

42. Veneer and inlay decoration of the second marquetry period, to designs by Robert Adam and executed by Messrs Chippendale and Haig 1772-1779. Veneers of rosewood, satinwood, kingwood, sycamore and harewood (sycamore dyed green with oxide of iron) were used on this secretaire chest. The ends are quartered rosewood enhanced with satinwood crossbanding and boxwood stringing; the secretaire drawer is crossbanded with satinwood, kingwood and rosewood around the panel of formal foliate marquetry which is further enhanced with surface etching, a method of decoration not used on English marquetry until this period. The doors bear quartered rosewood inserted with oval panels surrounded by entwined bands called 'guilloche' borders and Classical vases in fields of satinwood. The columns are decorated with honeysuckle motifs and the feet have a panel of satinwood over a single Greek key. A secretaire or secretary has a drawer which is hinged at the bottom and when pulled out falls to the horizontal to form a writing surface supported by two brass quadrants and reveals a set of small drawers and compartments similar to those in a bureau. Secretaires were particularly popular from c. 1770 to 1810.

43. A satinwood bonheur du jour or lady's writing table, c. 1790. In the manner of Thomas Sheraton's earlier designs, this table shows the effective use of quartered and crossbanded veneers and the absence of any marquetry. The finely tapered legs are panelled with a single line of boxwood stringing and it can be seen that they taper from the inside edges only to avoid a 'pin-toed' appearance. Half of the table top is hinged at the front edge and folds over to be supported by the drawer which when open reveals a pen and ink compartment at the side.

44. A rosewood cheveret or lady's writing table with portable book carrier, c. 1795. Like the bonheur du jour, this type of small table was extremely popular during the last fifteen years of the 18th century and the Sheraton period. This one shows the use of well figured, but not quartered, rosewood veneer panelled and bordered with fine stringing and satinwood crossbanding. The lower platform with a recessed front edge was a popular feature of the cheveret, and the ivory knobs and spade toe castors are original.

45. (Below) A mahogany sofa table, c. 1800. This is a typical example of the plainer but fashionable furniture being produced at this time. The triple reed edge to the top had become popular by the end of the century, and the standard ends well show the plain sweeping splay legs terminating in horizontal cup castors. Contemporary cheval mirrors (tall swivel dressing mirrors) had supports and legs of the same kind, and during the late 19th and early 20th centuries were often 'married' to later Regency sofa table tops which were old but not as valuable as the type illustrated here.

46. A mahogany Davenport writing desk, c. 1805, decorated with ebonised stringing. The name Davenport is alleged to derive from a Captain Davenport who first commissioned such a piece to be made at the end of the 18th century. The one illustrated has an unusual fold-over top, four-reed edges and curved feet in the Regency classic style. The cup castors are original.

47. A Regency period mahogany 'breakfast' table, c. 1805. Towards the end of the 18th century, tables to seat four, six or eight people for meals in less formal rooms than the dining room had become popular. The oval or rectangular tops were invariably supported on a centre column and splay legs. The late 18th century legs swept off the column as shown on the sofa table (plate 45) but after the turn of the century the curved leg with a knee became popular, growing more exaggerated as the Regency period progressed. The top has a single band of black stringing; the legs are carved in the manner of George Smith and terminate in original lion's paw castors.

48. A Regency period mahogany library table with drum top, c. 1810. Such tables became popular during the last half of the 18th century, but the ebonised inlay to drawers and legs, the ring-turned column, the pronounced swell to the knees of the legs and the lion's paw castors date the table as early 19th century.

49. A mid-Regency period card table of mahogany decorated with ebonised inlay of Classical motifs, c. 1815. The centre column and platform with the legs spreading from each corner was a popular form for side and centre tables of this period. The top swivelled on the frame and opened across it. This table shows early use of the carved acanthus leaf on the knees and castors.

50. A carved wood and gilt mirror in the Regency marine style, c. 1810. The use of marine subjects for furniture decoration became fashionable following successful campaigns at sea during the early 1800s, but declined after 1815. The style was revived to a minor extent after 1835 but the proportions of the later examples are generally more ponderous.

51. (Below left) A late 18th century mahogany dining chair with plain turned legs and an openwork back below an overhanging top rail which is typical of the late Hepplewhite and early Sheraton design for light and elegant dining chairs of this type.

52. (Below right) A mahogany dining chair, c. 1795-1800, showing early use of the reeded, turned and tapering leg. The back shows a considerable Classical influence, being made to represent an open scroll or banner supported by two Roman fasces. This type of design was much popularised by the architect Henry Holland.

53. A 'carving' and 'single' dining chair of a type most popular in the Midlands during the early part of the 19th century. Production of such chairs was plentiful at this time, and they were usually made in sets of up to twenty-four. Distinguishing features dating them before 1825 are the inside top back rail, the veneeered panel with brass inlayed stringing, the spiral turned centre bar from which they get the name 'rope-back', the degree of fineness in the turned front legs, and the moulded sides and arms.

54. An early 19th century turned leg sideboard, decorated with well-figured mahogany veneer, c. 1810. The pattern of the legs often matched that of contemporary dining chairs, and like them this form of sideboard remained popular in the provinces until 1825-1830.

55. An extremely fine mahogany wardrobe or gentleman's clothes press, c. 1785. The term 'clothes press' is used to describe large enclosed pieces in which linen is stored in sliding trays, rather than having room to hang above the section containing four drawers. Highly figured veneers of satinwood and mahogany are used to decorate the front of this piece for which suggested designs can be found in many contemporary pattern books. This wardrobe bears a maker's label on the back of both bottom and top parts and on the inside of one drawer (see plate 56).

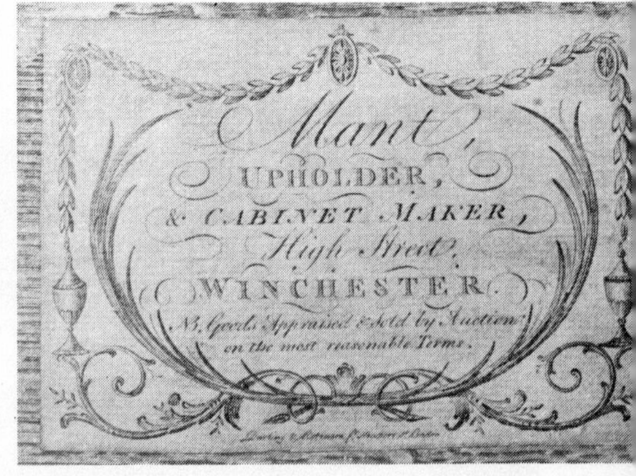

56. The maker's label attached to the wardrobe shown in plate 55 is that of Mant, High Street, Winchester. The labels of 18th century furniture manufacturers add a great deal of interest, if not value, to furniture of the period.

57. A Regency period pedestal-end sideboard and cellaret, c. 1815. The finely figured mahogany veneer is cross-banded and lined out with boxwood and gilt brass stringing. The semi-circular turned columns are an unusual feature and a mark of extra quality. The lion mask and ring handles are original; so too are the short curved front legs. It is usual to find turned back feet and curved front ones; by the end of the Regency period both front and back were turned. Occasionally the front feet are so exaggerated that the weight is taken by a block in the centre of the pedestal base.

58. A mahogany what-not, c. 1805. Designs for sets of square or rectangular shelves with a drawer or cupboard compartment at the base were divers from 1800 onward. The more typical example has each shelf separated by turned columns similar to those of the lower part in the illustration. This is unusual in the lyre shape supports at the top. The drawer retains a cock bead edge which is repeated on the end panels. The turned wood knobs are original; so too are the carved wood lion's paw feet at the front and the turned feet at the back.

59. A carved wood and gilt convex mirror, c. 1805. This type of mirror was introduced from France to England towards the end of the 18th century and by 1800 had become extremely popular. Good quality examples are invariably crested by an eagle with a ball and chain pendant from its beak. They were much advocated by Thomas Sheraton in his 'Cabinet Dictionary' of 1803 for the attractive light reflections created by the convex mirror plate. The illustration shows the inclusion of dolphins and bullrushes with a sea-horse at the base.

60. (Below left) A rosewood side table in the Classical style of the early Regency period, c. 1808. Charles Heathcote Tatham, Henry Holland and Thomas Hope were among the leaders of the Neo-classical style and its full impact can probably best be seen embodied in George Smith's 'A Collection of Designs for Household Furniture and Interior Decoration' (1808). The scrolling strap to the animal's breast and the formalised acanthus leaf below are two typical features often found in Smith's designs. The table is surmounted with a marble top and the back retains its original mirror plate. This type of furniture is often confused with that of twenty years later, but almost imperceptibly designs of the 1820s began to get heavier, the foliage thicker and the animals fatter.

61. (Below right) A detail of the carved support shown in plate 60.

62. (Left) A late Regency period cupboard with mirror glass back and shelf over, c. 1820. Referred to as a chiffonier, these were often made in pairs, and this one bears many features of the later Regency: the turned and reeded bun feet, the heavily lobed and beaded borders, the moulded side columns capped with formal acanthus leaf scroll, and the stylised lotus leaf at the base of each gilt metal support. The pierced brass gallery and the brass grill to the doors are original. Many later chiffoniers were made with solid wood panelled doors which, to increase their market value, have been removed and replaced with reproduction grills.

63. (Right) A late Regency period cabinet in the Classical style, c. 1822. The cabinet is veneered with kingwood and ebonised stringing and has a cornice more typical of the style of Thomas Hope; however, the freestanding columns to the base and the overall proportions are too heavy for the early Regency archaeological taste and, to support this, a design for a similar article was published in 1822 by Richard Brown.

64. A rosewood dining chair, c. 1828. This chair includes many features of the later Regency which were to set the scene for the William IV and early Victorian furniture designs: the double curved and overhanging back top rail, the formal tendril scroll under, the centre back splat pierced and carved with foliate motifs and the finely carved inverted lotus leaf cap to each front leg. The semi-circular baton front rail is unusual, but one or two unexpected features continued to appear on finer quality furniture until large scale mass-production took over.

65. The corner and drawer end of a mahogany chest of drawers, c. 1765. Here can be seen the development of the dovetail joints from those of the early 18th century (see plate 3). Note the end of the drawer front is rebated to receive the cock bead which runs all round the edge. When the drawer is closed (see lower drawer) the front is flush with the carcase leaving the cock bead proud up to one-eighth of an inch. This method of decorating drawer fronts continued into the early 1800s, but by the end of the 18th century, a single band of boxwood stringing became more popular until c. 1825.

66. A bird-cage platform shown with the top tilted. This top has an unusual framework of four runners instead of two. A lighter area and four bruises corresponding to the protruding column ends are clearly visible on the underside of the top, caused by close contact with the platform when the top is closed. Darker shading is where frequent dusting has created a dull shine. Such a combination of features is never successfully attained by the faker.

67. The corner and drawer end of a chest of drawers, c. 1805. This shows a good quality piece, the drawer linings of which are now mahogany rather than oak. The dovetails are cut much finer, and a line of ebony stringing has replaced the cock bead. The lion mask and ring handles are original, and the four-reed edge to the top supports this date.

68. (Left) A mahogany work table, c. 1795. The top has a narrow line of satinwood crossbanding and the drawer fronts are edged with stringing. The pendant handles as shown in fig. 64 are original and the legs can be seen to taper on the inside only.

69. (Below) The inside of the work box shown above. The evident alterations are described in detail on page 191.

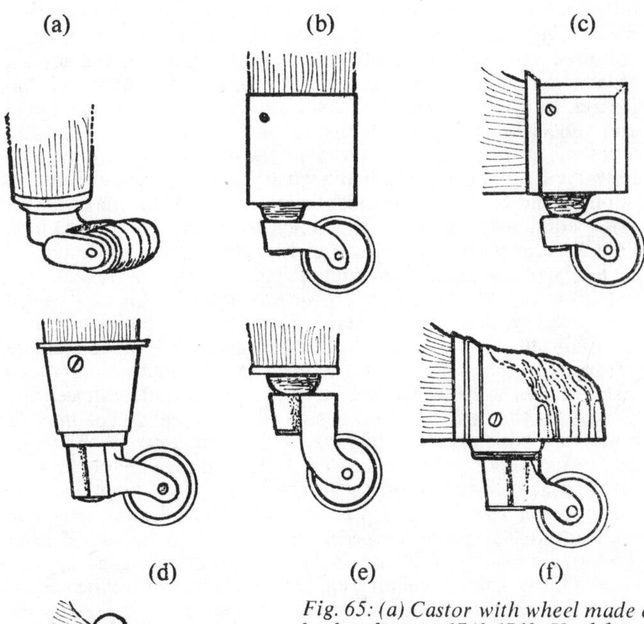

Fig. 65: (a) Castor with wheel made of leather discs, c. 1740-1760. Used for ball and claw feet and square untapered legs. (b) Square cup castor, c. 1760-1775, by which time it was generally made of brass. (c) The plain toe castor on the horizontal used for the spreading legs of the tripod and four splay table bases. From 1790 if tapered. (d) The tapered cup castor which with a top protruding lip often replaced the spade foot for turned and square legs, from 1785. (e) A small brass castor used on small pieces of furniture during the last quarter of the eighteenth century. (f) The lion's paw castor, 1800-1820, but a most popular replacement for later or reproduction furniture. (g) A typical late Regency stylised foliate cap castor, c. 1820-1835.

ally called faneer, because it was first produced by cutting across the grain, thus showing the 'fan' of the timber, rather than with the grain (see pages 29-30). The next development was the introduction from Holland of marquetry. This describes a decorative panel or border made up of several contrasting coloured veneers in intricate designs and applied to the carcase as a whole. There are two distinct types of marquetry of this period, see chart on page 194, and both these as well as parquetry and veneer in general continued as one of the most fashionable types of furniture decoration until the end of the seventeenth century. By the early 1700s marquetry and parquetry were less popular and by the 1730s most fashionable cabinet makers were using solid mahogany in preference to walnut veneer. During the Classical period of the later eighteenth century, the import of a variety of exotic timbers encouraged a revival of veneer and, to a lesser extent, marquetry. However, eighteenth century veneer of mahogany, satinwood, rosewood, etc., was generally cut along the grain, that is down the tree, rather than across, and contemporary marquetry also had a feature in its manufacture which distinguishes it from the earlier type. On seventeenth century marquetry the additional details of veins on leaves, feathers on birds etc., which appear to have been scribed on to the wood are, in fact, fine saw cuts, and are made more easily perceptible by the glue having risen through these cuts when the marquetry was applied. Eighteenth century classical period marquetry had such additional detail scribed or drawn on to the wood after the panel had been applied, giving an even finer, etched appearance. This was not done on English marquetry before the middle of the eighteenth century. The designs too were different: the eighteenth century version employing classical motifs, military trophies, shells and quarter fans rather than the scrolling vine, tendril and floral patterns which were popular in the seventeenth century. Quartering the veneer also became popular again, being made even more distinctive with the use of such woods as satinwood, mahogany and kingwood cut along the grain. A fine example of this can be seen in plate 43. To complete and frame the carefully selected and applied veneers, stringing and crossbanding were also reintroduced. These were found to be ideal for both fine and more ordinary furniture, as the insertion of a line of contrasting colour wood to a plain surface, such as boxwood to mahogany, and an edge of crossbanding immediately gave a fashionable appearance to a mediocre article. Herringbone stringing in its earlier form was not popular: instead, variations of chequer stringing were sometimes used. Both these and panels of wood marquetry went out of fashion towards the end of the century and remained so until after 1850 when their revival continued until c. 1910. During the Regency period, burr veneers were extremely popular, and after 1815 panels of buhl work were used on the finest furniture. The word buhl describes panels of brass and tortoiseshell inlay produced in the same way as marquetry: thin sheets of each material are glued together and the required design, generally of intricate scrolls and foliage, is cut through both diagonally; the glue is melted and the designs and materials can then be interchanged. The two alternatives of background or decoration material thus provided are known as buhl and counter-buhl, and furniture to be decorated in this way was often made in pairs to take both. Folding tea and card tables, wall cabinets, chiffoniers and bookcases are typical examples. Red, deep yellow and green tortoiseshell could be obtained by varying the colour of the surface to which the buhl panel was applied. This method of decoration was first used in England during the late seventeenth century, and derives its name from the originator in France, Andre Charles Boule, see chart on page 194. It did not receive the popularity in England it gained on the Continent at this time, and was little used in England after the first quarter of the eighteenth century. In 1815, however, another Frenchman, Louis Gaigneur, opened premises in London, and supplied to the Prince Regent a writing table decorated with buhl. From then on it remained fashionable in varying degrees, terminating in a deluge of mass production in the 1870s.

THE CONTINUING INFLUENCE OF PAST STYLES

The structure of furniture production, which had become established during preceding periods, began to expand visibly through the short reign of William IV and the early years of the Victorian era. Equally, the pattern of design development apparent from the sixteenth century, with the introduction, improvement and inevitable over-elaboration of a style followed by a modified revival of an earlier fashion, can be seen to continue throughout the Victorian and early Edwardian periods. Both structure and pattern were however made considerably more complex and difficult to chronicle by the advent of mechanisation which enabled the production of a greater range of quality and variety of styles than ever before.

The more architectural elements of the classical antique, popularised during the Regency period (the period when fashion was influenced by the young Prince George rather than purely the nine years of constitutional Regency) by the work of such men as Henry Holland, Thomas Hope, George Smith, George Bullock and Richard Brown (see plate 63) continued to dominate the more masculine apartments in the fashionable houses well into the 1840s. Examples of its use can be found dating from later in the nineteenth century but they cannot be regarded as typical of the then contemporary fashions. These designs are referred to as Grecian or Egyptian, the latter being the more truly descriptive, and can be recognised by such motifs as the unbroken pediment, curved corner brackets, formalised lotus and acanthus leaf capping to columns and side supports, and the continued popularity of the sarcophagus shape. One visible change which occurred during the 1820-1840 period was that the 'bas-relief' carving of the decorative motifs became heavier and, later, even cumbersome. The timber most popular for the construction of furniture made in this style was Honduras, San Domingo and Mexican mahogany, french polished to a glossy finish and reddish colour.

Also at this time three other headings describe the sources of inspiration for furniture designers and architects. They are the 'Old French', the 'Medieval' and the 'Elizabethan'. To begin with, designs in the Old French taste were based essentially on those of the Louis XIV period, but during the 1830s practically all the important designs of eighteenth and early nineteenth-century France were employed. The taste became apparent in two ways. Firstly the popularity of buhl (brass inlay) marquetry, the finest of which is said to have come from the workshops of Louis Gaigneur in England during the later Regency period, developed with the increasing demand for long, low wall cabinets of ebonised wood decorated with panels of buhl and further enriched with cast and chased metal mounts often surrounding porcelain panels bearing paintings of classical scenes. This type of cabinet, in every conceivable form, continued in favour throughout the rest of the century, carrying all types of decoration from high relief carving of allegorical subjects to the finest and most tastefully executed inlay, marquetry and other veneer work. Secondly, in 1827 Phillip and Benjamin Dean Wyatt were responsible for the redecoration of Crockford's Club, stressing their obvious delight in the deeply curving frames for chairs and settees, luxurious drapes of richly braided and fringed velours, and elaborate stucco work to walls and ceilings. This was indeed the origin of the curved-leg and oval-backed parlour and dining chairs which today seem to typify 'Victoriana' and which in the past have often been misdescribed as 'Queen Anne'.

The Medieval taste is also referred to as Gothic, for it is

this aspect which formed the basis of many of the purer medieval furniture designs. Gothic, too, had been the subject of considerable renewed interest during the later Regency period, with ecclesiastical motifs providing the main theme. The patterns of Perpendicular, Curvilinear, Geometric and Decorated period church architecture are all represented, with the quatrefoil and lancet window shapes and crocket decoration to spires and towers being among the most popular. These patterns were employed for both the basic shape and the decoration of all types of furniture as well as architecture during the 1840s and 1850s. The finest example by one of the leading exponents of this taste, Augustus Welby Pugin, is the decoration of the Houses of Parliament (ceremonially opened in 1852).

Furniture which reflected the more distinct 'Medieval' features might have battlements, portcullis, simulated masonry and iron or steel strapwork incorporated with the ecclesiastical decor of Gothic.

The 'Elizabethan' design was purely Victorian in concept, for it shows the fascination the Victorians had with the original English renaissance or Romanesque period, and their apparent love of the overdecorated pastiche. Rooms were panelled in oak and furnished with heavily carved buffets, cupboards, sideboards, tables and chairs in such profusion as could never have been envisaged previously. Much of the carving depicts Victorianised Elizabethan figures in romantic settings surmounted by sentries, guardian angels often in apparent distress, supported by bacchanalian torsos amid Italian and French style curves and scrolls.

William IV, 1830-1837

William IV was a kindly man, given to long speeches, and known to his subjects as the 'Sailor King' through his eleven-year career in the Royal Navy. But he showed little enthusiasm for altering the course of political history and even less inclination to influence the design and decoration of English furniture. That the king was favourably disposed to the passing of the Reform Bill (1831-2) of Earl Grey can only be said to give him the remotest connections with the subsequent development of the furniture industry in Great Britain, and it is in the wider aspects of social environment that the reasons for change may be found.

By the end of the William IV period (1830-1837) furniture manufacture in England had grown into a vast industry employing thousands of highly skilled and specialised workers.

THE EARLY VICTORIAN PERIOD

In 1837 William IV died, and on 28th June 1838 his niece Victoria was crowned queen. Victoria, born in 1819, was daughter of Edward, Duke of Kent, fourth son of George III. She married Albert, Prince of Saxe-Coburg and Gotha (the Prince Consort) and bore him nine children. Until her death in 1901 Victoria reigned over a country whose history was marked by unequalled industrial development, spasmodic economic uncertainty, and a long series of wars and campaigns in various parts of an expanding empire. Following the death of Prince Albert in 1861, Queen Victoria was seen less and less as a public figure, and the Prince and Princess of Wales took a more active part in state affairs, especially those of a social nature. Victoria's was a reign of iron, steel, the harnessing of steam, gas and electricity; of the development of travel, large hotels, postage and newspapers; of telegraphs, tramcars and underground railways.

Among all these certainly not the least to flourish was the furniture industry, which by 1850 had at its disposal the earliest type of steam-powered carving machinery, an invention which was to change forever the production of furniture and its allied industries. However, the amazing variety of designs which sprang comparatively suddenly into prominence during the fifteen years prior to the Great Exhibition of 1851 can be accounted for in many other ways: the rise in population from five and a half million in 1702 to eighteen million; vastly increased prosperity for a large portion of the community; improvements in transport and communication, and the Industrial Revolution.

The Victorian age was one of the greatest periods of religious zeal in our history, and this often smothering, sometimes pious enthusiasm did a great deal to keep alive the demand for ecclesiastical decoration, better described in the title of one of the many works by A. W. Pugin, *The True Principles of Pointed or Christian Architecture* (1841). Equally, as a natural reaction to the permissiveness of the Regency society, exposure of the female form was kept to a minimum, waists were 'straight-laced' and skirts once again became voluminous; being made of rich and invariably heavy materials they were also dangerous to the delicate pieces of furniture of the late eighteenth and early nineteenth centuries. So not only taste, but also fashion, decreed that at least free-standing or 'occasional' furniture should be more substantial. During the latter part of the century even the legs of tables, chairs, settees, pianofortes, chimney pieces and shelves were covered with material—if not upholstered then draped with fitted covers with deep fringing.

A considerable encouragement to the Elizabethan taste was the appearance and enormous popularity after 1814 of the romantic novels by Sir Walter Scott and a host of factual books on this early period of English history. However, this interest was more an entertainment than a thirst for precise knowledge, a supposition substantiated by the fact that countless examples of authentic early English furniture were cut up and used either whole or in part to make new pieces which would fit more suitably into the fashionable Victorian house. This practice continued to such an extent that it was possible to visit premises where large stocks of Elizabethan furniture parts such as chest fronts, bed-posts, drawers and drawer fronts and other decorative sections could be bought already mutilated or dismembered to order. After the commissioned cabinet-maker had done his work the finished article was often further decorated by members of the family pursuing the latest pastime of wood-carving. This frightening hobby gained rapid popularity after the showing of work produced by the Warwick School of Carving at the Great Exhibition (fig. 66).

For the student of furniture it is invariably apparent that any period of excess, whether of plainness or overdecoration, is accompanied by an unsettled state of the nation's political, social and economic situation. Thus the 1840s with their uncertainty and unrest in all these spheres produced a formidable mixture of design and decoration flung together as if in an attempt to find satisfaction in at least the decorative arts. The attempt was doomed through the incompatibility of the components. This observation should only be applied to the extreme examples or prestige pieces of the period made for a wealthy minority; for some fine quality and aesthetically pleasing furniture was also made at this time. But it is the fashion leaders which formed the basis of style for the less expensive pieces and which always tend to be shown as truly representative of any given period.

English furniture on display at the Crystal Palace in 1851 illustrated the ultimate fancies of designers and decorators, and the supreme heights of technical achievement in the hands of skilled manufacturers. It also reflected the spirit of England at the time for it was stated in many reviews that works of art from any part of the world and of any period in history could be as well if not better made by English craftsmen. This overriding passion to prove best in imitation left little space for any

Fig. 66: An oak sideboard with triple mirror back, in the style of the Warwick School of Carving. The columns are carved with fruit pendants in the Grinling Gibbons manner, while the borders and cornice show a neo-classical influence (c. 1865).

evidence of our hereditary invention of the original as far as the decoration of furniture is concerned. However, the concept of the Crystal Palace was certainly original, and its design the basic idea of one Englishman, Joseph Paxton.

The Great Exhibition

The idea of holding public exhibitions of various fields of the decorative arts was not a new one. As early as 1757 the Society of Arts had offered prizes for the best examples of such wares as carpets, porcelain and tapestry, and exhibited the entries. In 1762 the Royal Academy of Painting was established and since then numerous branches of industry had shown interest in this type of competitive display. However, until the mid nineteenth century, enthusiasm for art exhibitions in general was

Fig. 67: A sideboard of similar proportions to that illustrated in fig. 66, being decorated in the Classical style of the later Victorian period. The panelled effect to the columns and frieze is created by gauged lines instead of inlaid stringing, and was a popular method of decorating slate chimney and mantel pieces, also the slate and marble clocks which became so popular during the last thirty years of the nineteenth century. The lines were often ebonised or gilded.

much greater in France than in England. Under the leadership of Henry Cole, the Society of Arts was persuaded to organise three annual exhibitions from 1847 to 1849. Following the success of the last, a deputation from the Society met the Lord Mayor of London with plans for holding an International Exhibition in a suitable position, ultimately Hyde Park. Cole obtained the patronage of Prince Albert whose interest was aroused to the extent that he contributed far more than had been expected and took most of the credit for its considerable success.

The meeting with the Lord Mayor was well attended by more than four hundred wealthy bankers and merchants and, according to an eyewitness account, the atmosphere was conducive to optimism as to the availability of funds. So until the preparation of plans for the actual building commenced, no major setbacks had been encountered. A month was allocated as time for receipt of all drawings, and over 230 competitors submitted plans. Unfortunately none of these plans was considered suitable, so the Building Committee devised a plan of their own. This too was found to be impracticable, but seven days before the deadline the firm of Fox and Henderson prepared and finalised detailed drawings of a plan by Joseph Paxton to build an enormous pavilion of glass—the Crystal Palace

The Crystal Palace was a vast structure of iron and glass enclosing approximately nineteen acres of Hyde Park, and tall enough to include the huge elm trees growing there. The galleries and upper bays were to provide a third as much space again to help accommodate the 15,000 exhibitors from all over the world. The main entrance led into a huge vaulted transept with domed roof and galleries all round. To right and left of this there extended the two huge wings of the building constructed in three graduated floors with the flags of all nations flying round its borders. Thirty miles of iron frame formed the roof, and 900,000 square feet of glass were used to form the shell. To allay any fears of its structural safety eight-ton wagons of cannonballs were hauled up and down the aisles, and companies of troops marched in closed ranks around the bays. After the Exhibition the Palace was rebuilt at Sydenham and there remained until 1936 when it was burnt to the ground.

Financial success was assured, for apart from over £60,000 from public subscription and £40,000 from the sale of season tickets (£3 for gentlemen, £2 for ladies), Spicer and Clowes paid £32,000 for rights to print the catalogues, and Schweppes paid £55,000 for the rights to supply refreshments. In the event over £75,000 worth of soft drinks and light food was sold. After the first three weeks the entrance fee was lowered to one shilling weekdays and half-a-crown and five shillings at weekends thus encouraging more than six million people to visit and view the displays. These were segregated into four classes: Sculpture and Fine Arts, Raw Materials, Machinery, and Manufacture. There were over one million exhibits and the Exhibition was open from 1st May until 7th October 1851.

Although the Crystal Palace closed in October, the interest it had aroused did not die, and the great age of International Exhibitions had begun. This brief account of the 1851 Exhibition should demonstrate why our furniture history became quite so complex during this period. All the countries participating brought fresh ideas of design and decoration, each to have its own impact on the desires of the English buying public; vast amounts of money were in circulation; steam-powered machinery was revolutionising production; one particular fashion was no longer the overriding taste decreed by one class of the community and for the first time fashionable furniture to a variety of styles could be bought direct from a shop instead of being made specifically to designs in a book.

The hall-stand

With one or two exceptions, the basic items of furniture in the middle-class house did not change in character until the 1850s, after which time more distinct developments can be seen. What innovations there were prior to the middle of the century can best be related to some changes in social behaviour and the houses themselves.

The hall-stand first appeared during the later years of the Regency period as a turned post, free-standing, with arms to take cloaks and hats. It was not until the entrance hall gained prominence in middle-class as well as upper-class houses that this useful article became so much in demand. In the masses of smaller houses the hall was often narrow, serving as access to all the downstairs and basement rooms, as well as the staircase and landing for the upper floors. To make the stand more useful without increasing its size it was placed against the wall, a shelf was built mid-way up the column, and a drawer compartment was fitted below. Following this the arms were made to extend from either side and a mirror was placed in the centre. Umbrella and cane divisions were built on to the sides of the drawer and iron drip-trays were sunk in the base. And so developed the hall-stand which, made from a variety of materials, by the end of the century could be found in practically every house in the country (fig. 68).

The miles of stoutly built terraced houses erected in all major cities and towns during the Victorian age are evidence of the suddenly enormous section of moderately wealthy middle-class society. Each house had a basement with usually more than two floors above and was considered incomplete without at least one resident maid or servant. Thus furniture had to be produced for all these new servants' quarters, as well as spare bedrooms and attics, as every available space was utilised to its fullest extent. Apart from the need for so much mass-produced furniture in fashionable if simple taste, two other reasons can be said to account for the increase in the variety

Fig. 68 (left): A design for a hall-stand of which there were numerous variations (c. 1850-1875). The development of this piece of furniture is discussed on pages 123-4.

Fig. 69 (right): A mid-Victorian carved wood and gilt console table with a pier glass over in the classical style. Examples of such fixtures can be found in an enormous variety of designs. Many had much lower tables suitable for the arrangement of large plants and flower displays in front of the long mirror.

of articles required for the well-furnished house: the vogue for indoor plants and conservatories, and the increased popularity of smoking.

Indoor plants

The Victorians developed a passion for gardens in general and foliage in particular, and large glass conservatories were added to the exterior of bigger houses to provide all-the-year-round floral displays or 'winter gardens'. Such constructions were obviously impossible for the smaller houses and so landings, halls and bays in morning rooms had glass casements strategically placed to provide the effect of ever luxurious greenery against the light from inside and a grand window display from outside. It was soon found that many of the popular plants would thrive without this internal greenhouse and the age of the free-standing pot-plant had begun. The present-day demand for all types of house-plants can therefore be seen as a revival of a fashion which ceased during the period of the two world wars.

Just as now, the Victorians required containers for their individual plants and an enormous number of jardinieres and plant stands appeared in a variety of styles. Two of the most popular were, first, the circular container with metal liner and bodywork of cane panels, supported on three curving legs and with platform below, often gilded or painted in the classical style, and second, the rectangular box-top table on centre turned or fluted column and platform base, the top having the metal lined 'well' covered by a lift-off panel thus enabling its alternative use as an occasional table.

The smoking room and the parlour

The second reason for new pieces of furniture was the increased popularity of smoking among the upper and middle classes. Houses had 'smoking rooms' and 'towers' set aside as apartments unentered by ladies. The tower room was a three-quarter circular room attached to the upper outside corner or other extremity of a house giving a romantic castle appearance. This architectural feature was by no means confined to larger houses, and many examples can be seen on 'high street' corner buildings in both large cities and small provincial towns, as well as on country mansions. The smoking room required pipe stands and racks, cigar cabinets and cases, smokers' compendiums and a host of smaller gadgets deemed necessary for correct smoking procedure.

Apart from the exclusion of female company from smoking rooms the Victorian family became a much closer unit, with great importance attached to individual hobbies, such as flower and model making, painting, and compiling scrapbooks, being pursued together, as well as musical and recital evenings and family parties. Most of these activities took place in the 'morning room' or parlour and it is during the middle of the century that the parlour suite became most popular. This consisted of a three-seat settee, two armchairs, one of which was larger for the gentleman, and a set of six to ten single chairs (without arms).

The idea of this type of chair, as distinct from a dining chair, had started in the late eighteenth century when concerts in the music room or recitals in the library were held in the bigger houses and attended by large groups of people. The chairs were similar in size and design to the currently fashionable dining chairs but the backs were inclined at a greater degree to give added comfort. During the early years of the Victorian age the distinction between dining-room and parlour chairs continued, the former remaining substantial and becoming heavy in appearance, the latter following the latest design fashion, strongly favouring the 'Old French' influence with curving legs and loop backs. However, the less wealthy households had to combine the dining-room and the morning or family room, and most dining chairs produced during the remainder of the century were made suitable for both: strong enough for boisterous, though well-disciplined, mealtimes, with upright backs and fully upholstered and often deeply buttoned seats, and decorative enough to comply with the current fashionable designs.

Dining tables

By the 1840s two distinct types of table had become favourites for the dining-room. The first was the circular 'Loo' table first popularised during the Regency period for the card game of that name, and the second was the extendable or 'draw-leaf' dining table first introduced into England during the late Elizabethan period. The basic construction of the Loo table, with the top supported by a large centre column on rectangular or triform platform base, carved feet and castors, remained the same until the 1860s, being varied by different patterns of decoration. However, during the 1840s it was running concurrently with a new revival of the mid eighteenth-century support, the deeply curved quadruped or tripod base. This rapidly became carved and pierced, and was generally made of solid rosewood and later walnut. Plain and shaped oval-top centre tables also became popular at this time, so too did the swivel and fold-over top tea and card tables, all on the open curved-leg base rather than having the legs placed at each corner.

The most popular version of the extending or draw-leaf dining table was generally made of mahogany and had either semi-circular or severe D-shaped ends. These were made to pull out on long interfitting rails to leave space in the centre for the additional sections of table top. The legs were invariably turned and tapering, with large bulbous flutes. By the end of the century the extension was achieved by turning a crank on the end of a long spirally threaded metal rod. During the first quarter of the twentieth century such tables were often supported on cabriole-style legs, the deeply curved knees

Fig. 70: A conversation settee of triform scrolling shape, the deep buttoned armrest supported by turned columns and scroll-carved ends. A deep fringe conceals the legs on this example (c. 1855—but it should be noted that such pieces continued to be made for the next thirty years).

carved with a mixture of mid eighteenth-century motifs and terminating in claw and ball feet.

Considering the expansive and revolutionary times in which they lived, it is not at all surprising that the Victorians were obsessed by the succession of inventions for personal aid and household decoration to an almost absurd degree. Elaborate mechanical devices were patented to assist the lives of the widest possible cross-section of the community. From aspiring deep sea divers and aviators, smokers and drinkers, cooks and bottle-washers, to the partially and totally invalided, there were aids purporting to guarantee success, assistance or cure. What is interesting is that out of this confusion came only one or two extremely useful ideas—for example the combination hall-stand (see fig. 68), and the two-seater 'conversation' settee with a small circular tray-top table built in the centre (see fig. 70), while there continued enormous demand for a surprisingly small range of standard articles which although they received all manner of current decoration, remained basically the same in structure and use.

The chiffonier (plate 99) became one of the most popular dining-room or parlour wall pieces, together with the well established pedestal sideboard for larger houses. As the century progressed, these two were often combined to make a capacious enclosed cupboard below a variety of elaborate superstructures. Depending on the style these might consist of shelves, brackets, small cupboards and large overhanging cornices around one central and sometimes several side mirror panels. The popularity of a mirror back between the supporting pedestals *below* the top of a sideboard of the later Regency and William IV period declined during the Victorian age.

NEW TECHNIQUES AND MASS PRODUCTION

T. B. Jordan—mechanised production

One of the most important innovations to affect the decoration of furniture was the invention and success of a wood-carving machine first produced by T. B. Jordan in 1845. This enabled one man to produce several pieces of identical decoration at the same time. Thus a new form of mass production emerged. Instead of several craftsmen working on different parts of one piece of furniture, it was now conceivable that those same men could produce, with the aid of machine sawing, planing and now carving, many parts for many pieces of furniture in the same time it took to do the one single operation. Maximum production from minimum labour became the supposed essential ingredient of any Victorian industry. Unfortunately, in the furniture trade the machine was allowed, for a time, to take over from taste and design. This is well illustrated by much of the furniture produced during the 1851 to 1870 period, where it can be seen from the decoration that the machine operator was at all times attempting to prove the superiority of technical achievement within the scope of his machine.

This situation was further complicated in certain cases by examples of the Warwick School of Carving and its imitators making obvious their one aim to prove their superiority with a carving chisel to anything that a machine could produce. This period was certainly the great age of overdecoration on even the more modest pieces of household furniture. The most popular timbers were oak and walnut, the latter being used in the solid as well as cut for veneer. Drawer linings on better-quality furniture were made mostly of mahogany, the rest being of any cheaper woods, usually pine and deal. Barley-sugar twist turning became popular, combined with under-cut cups with pendant borders and tapering reeded columns. In this way three fashionable designs from different periods of the seventeenth and eighteenth centuries were often incorporated in one article (plate 98). Pierced fret-work also became extremely popular at this time, as did panels of marquetry. Fret borders were used as galleries at the back edges of shelves to prevent items slipping off, and below the front edges as pure decoration. Panels of fine fret-work were often backed with coloured silk and used for doors or decoration to the fronts of harmoniums and pianos.

For the first time mechanised production, new and improved techniques of surface decoration and an apparently inexhaustible imagination regarding the use of all kinds of alternative materials gave the manufacturers of furniture and household fitments the means to provide their less wealthy clients with deceptively good facsimiles of the finest examples of contemporary design and construction. Unfortunately the use of inferior materials gave rise to a rapid dilapidation, and the poor-quality furniture of this type which has survived to the present day can be easily recognised by its badly worn and loose jointed appearance. Certainly one of the reasons that so much upholstered furniture of the early and mid Victorian period is now found to be in a rotting and worm-ridden condition is that in striving for cheapness with good effect, bad and often infected stuffings were used instead of the much more expensive cleaned and curled horse-hair.

Upholstered furniture

By 1833 quantities of coiled springs for chairs, settees, sofas and bedding were being produced in Birmingham, and it was from this period on that fully sprung seats became popular. During the eighteenth century the upholsterer took into account the design of the chair or seat he had to cover, using the minimum amount of filling to accentuate the contours of the piece. By the 1840s the seat frame became more of a vehicle for the maximum amount of plush upholstery the craftsman could apply, thus giving it the appearance of a bloated marsh-mallow on legs which, by the 1850s, were themselves hidden by deep fringe. During this latter period it became universally popular to secure these huge amounts of springs, stuffing, lining and top cover with deep buttoning, giving a dimpled but difficult to clean surface. The Chesterfield-type settee (see fig. 71) is the best example of this. Deep buttoning was not new at this time, but its earlier use had been limited to the more expensive upholstered furniture.

Prior to the use of coiled springs, the basic webbing on a seat frame extended over the top of the rails; following their introduction the webbing was stretched across the bottom edge of the seat rails to support the springs. It was common practice on better-quality pieces to cover the underneath with neatly fitting black or neutral material, known as 'bottom-

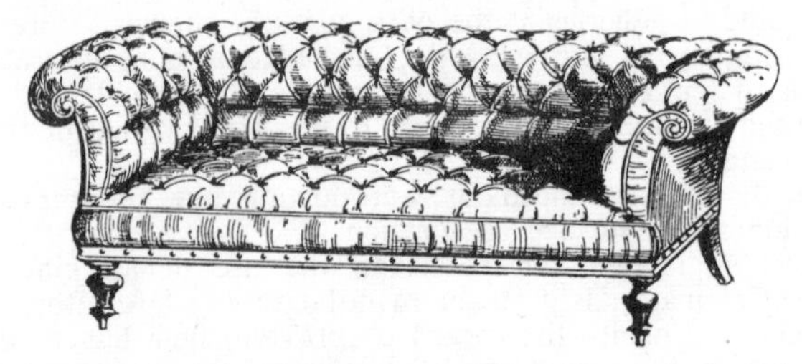

Fig. 71: A library or hall sofa, similar in form to the Chesterfield settee. This type of seat became popular for billiard rooms and gentlemen's clubs during the last forty years of the nineteenth century (and later).

canvassing'. By the mid 1830s the method of 'finishing' the edges of the top cover round the seat rails by 'brass-nailing' had gone out of fashion. (This was the application of large brass dome-headed nails along the edge of the material to hide the small less regularly placed fixing tacks.) Instead, machine-made braid or 'gimp' was used, being fixed with small nails called gimp-pins.

Contemporary publications

While it was now possible for the manufacturer to produce several identical articles at one time, it was becoming increasingly difficult for the moderately wealthy but more discerning client to acquire custom-made furniture. Furniture could now be bought, ready made, in the high street shop, and many of the current books of designs available were used by their authors as a means of critical comment on contemporary bad taste. There were, by the middle of the nineteenth century, several distinct categories of these publications.

The first important type continued the format which became so popular in England during the eighteenth century—the pattern book. Probably the best-known of the early pattern books is *The Gentleman and Cabinet Maker's Director,* by Thomas Chippendale, first published in 1754. This was followed by similar important works including *The Cabinet Maker and Upholsterer's Guide,* by George Hepplewhite, in 1788, and it is evident that until the end of the eighteenth century these pattern books were produced by practising cabinet-makers or at least by those having close connections with a workshop, as in the case of Thomas Sheraton and *The Cabinet and Upholsterer's Drawing book,* published in three parts from 1791 to 1794.

During the eighteenth century it was considered increasingly important for architects to design interior fittings and furniture, thus by the end of the century the pattern book was no longer within the realms of cabinet-makers alone, but a method of portraying ideas for fashionable designs by talented and aesthetically minded patrons of the arts, writers and others so inclined. In 1807 such a patron, Thomas Hope, published *Household Furniture and Interior Decoration,* taking some inspiration from the architect Henry Holland. From this time on the pattern book can be segregated from the cabinet-makers' catalogues, which by the 1850s were being produced by all the leading manufacturers and showrooms as illustrated inventories of their currently available merchandise. Designs portrayed in the pattern books of the more influential designers were closely followed by the manufacturers, and their catalogues were evidence to the buying public of the firm's ability to keep up to date with the latest style.

In 1833 John C. Loudon published the *Encyclopedia of Cottage, Farm and Villa Architecture and Furniture* and produced a third form of reference book for the nineteenth-century and present-day enthusiast. This work and subsequent similar books presented a survey of available furniture and design with enormously detailed and often critical texts accompanying the copious illustrations. It was in this medium that many members of the Arts and Crafts movement found considerable freedom of expression later in the century, as well as in the rapidly growing number of regular publications and journals. These, and of course the catalogues to the many exhibitions, provide yet another invaluable source of information concerning the furniture industry and its background.

To the average citizen keen enough to browse through or even purchase a copy it meant little more than a glimpse of the sort of furniture he was unlikely ever to possess, and the knowledge that he either agreed or disagreed with the writer. However, the dogmatic individual and the poorer classes had an alternative source of supply; the second-hand shops or 'furniture brokers' as they were then called. These shops, which sprang up in large numbers in towns and cities throughout the land, catered for an increasing section of the community whose economic situation changed frequently, as well as for seekers of the authentic antique. Furniture of pine or deal, painted in imitation of better timbers, in pastel colours, or left plain, was the most used for servants' quarters and lesser bedrooms, and was produced in large quantities. On reaching a higher financial status, a family might well change much of this, and the occasional family heirloom relegated to an attic, for better quality furniture bought from a furnishing store, disposing of the original to a broker.

The structure of the furniture trade

Furniture stores were generally showrooms for goods made elsewhere, often from a variety of sources: iron bedsteads from Birmingham, turned fruitwood chairs from High Wycombe, fine mahogany, walnut and rosewood cabinets from London and Lancaster. Higher still in the social scale were the showrooms displaying goods made under the supervision of the proprietors, and at the very top were the shops of great names in the furniture industry. These were the fashion leaders, the publishers of catalogues advertising ready-made or custom-built pieces for the wealthiest families or 'carriage trade', a term descriptive of those patrons affording coach-house and stable property in a city. The firms were often long established, employing the finest craftsmen in the land, their name being an automatic guarantee of the best quality product. Among them Messrs. Gillow, Smee, Holland, Crace, and Arrowsmith should be mentioned. Many other firms specialised in whole-sale trade, and still more combined the two, with specific warehouses for wholesale and export display, as well as retail showrooms.

The establishment of large workshops under the ownership of a master craftsman or merchant began long before the nineteenth century, as can be seen from the records of Thomas Seddon who, in the 1780s, employed over three hundred journeymen. Nor was it a Victorian idea for master craftsmen of different branches of the trade to form partnerships, establish a shop or warehouse and undertake to supply their clients with everything connected with house furnishing. What did occur was, as previously stated, a decline in the production of custom-made pieces compared to the tremendous rise in mass production for the middle and lower classes, and a decline in the employment of journeymen in favour of the retained employee. The term 'journeyman' is derived from the French *journée*, a day's work; thus a journeyman might be employed on a piece-work basis, certainly owning his own tools. This is very much an oversimplification to illustrate a point in this brief text, for a complicated system of craft guilds and fraternities between journeymen or yeomen and merchants had existed since the fourteenth century. 'Journeyman' as a title is used to distinguish between a qualified workman and an apprentice.

One rather pathetic result of mechanisation in the furniture industry was the worsening plight of the self-employed 'part' maker. By the end of the eighteenth century it was not uncommon for larger workshops to commission a number of furniture parts such as chair rails, to be made by the urban equivalent of the 'cottage industry' worker. Such people were found in the East End of London and in other major cities, the prices for their work being protected by an ethical sense of responsibility within the trade on the side of the master craftsmen. The advent of machinery made such loyalty economically impossible, and during the mid nineteenth century the 'garret-masters', as they were known, could be seen hawking their wares from push-carts piled with a week's produce, desperate to sell in order to acquire more raw materials.

Papier-mâché

The tremendous demand for furniture in the nineteenth century may be better appreciated with reference to the increase in population. In 1500 the total population was just under five millions; by the year 1800 it had risen to nine millions; and by 1850 it had almost doubled again to just under eighteen millions. In 1851, the year of the Great Exhibition, nearly fifty thousand people were employed in the two main branches of the furniture industry, cabinet-making and upholstery. It is therefore not surprising that as well as new methods of manufacture, new materials were constantly being tried, either for genuine improvement or for the sake of pure sensationalism. Furniture of glass and coal can be safely placed in the latter category whereas modern techniques used in the production of already known materials can be recognised as genuine improvement.

Among these papier-mâché must rate high, for although first patented in England in 1772 by Henry Clay it did not become universally popular until the Victorian period. Literally translated 'papier-mâché' means pulped paper and the French product of that name used paper in this state for its manufacture; but Clay's method of production was very different to the French. Sheets of paper were placed over a mould, each one being well pasted to the next, and when dry the shape thus formed was baked to make it extremely hard. Clay was careful to distinguish between his product and true papier-mâché by naming it 'paper ware', but by the 1830s the firm of Jennens and Bettridge apparently decided that the original French name sounded much better even if it was not a true description of the product, and from then on both the cheaper pulped paper and paper ware have been called papier-mâché.

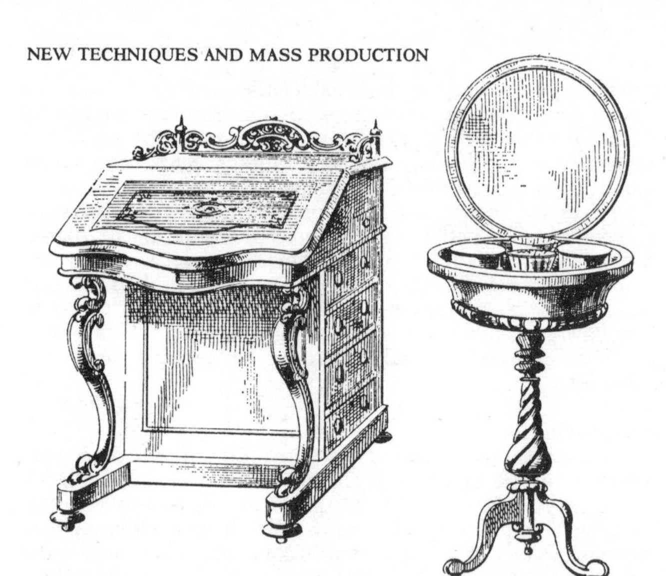

Fig. 72 (left): A mid nineteenth-century Davenport writing desk showing the very popular 'triple C' scroll free-standing supports on each front edge. The Davenport is discussed in greater detail on page 83.

Fig. 73 (right): A mid-Victorian teapoy, examples of which were constructed to this design in mahogany, rosewood or walnut, depending on the quality and cost. Teapoys or standing caddies, which became popular during the early years of the nineteenth century, were highly decorative free-standing pieces of furniture. The top contained two, three or four tea compartments, a glass bowl for mixing and blending the tea and another for sugar. The heavily lobed underpart and spiral baluster stem date this example from c. 1865.

The popularity of papier-mâché during the period 1835 to 1870 is substantiated by the large variety of articles made in this way still to be found in all parts of the country. From tea trays—sometimes in sets of three or four in graduating sizes topped with a matching high-sided bread basket—to writing boxes (plate 111), lap-desks (plate 112), work-tables, tilt-top tables, chairs and even foot and head boards for bedsteads, no article was left untried for the art of the papier-mâché maker. There were essentially two processes involved before a piece of papier-mâché was finished—construction and decoration. The surface of the plain or 'blank' article was found to be most suitable for the application of 'japanning' or lacquer work, the background of which was usually black, although all the other colours normally associated with this type of decoration were occasionally used. In the case of production from the larger factories in Birmingham and Wolverhampton, manufacture and decoration were carried out in the same establishment while there were numerous smaller works specialising in just decoration, buying the blanks from other similar-size workshops.

Earlier examples show the use of gold in dust, leaf or paint form combined with coloured enamels or paints as the most important ingredients of the decoration. In 1825 however, the application of paper-thin pieces of pearl-shell, known as mother-of-pearl, was introduced by George Souter who worked for Jennens and Bettridge. The shell was applied to the surface of the lacquer and painted with varnish to the required pattern. An acid solution was then applied and the unwanted portions of the shell, unprotected by the varnish, were eaten away leaving the effect of a delightful and deeply translucent insertion to the surface. It soon became apparent that earlier as well as contemporary panels of various materials could be incorporated into articles of papier-mâché, so too could coloured engravings and prints, and the surface was ideal for painted scenes of all manner of subjects—flowers and romantic landscapes being among the most popular.

Because the basic shapes of papier-mâché pieces remained much the same until the late 1870s, the various methods of decoration are frequently the best guide to the approximate date of origin. As a generalisation, the more varied the materials and ingredients applied to and incorporated in the surface, the later the piece is likely to be. Earlier pieces often bore excessive amounts of decoration but the materials used consisted of those normally found on contemporary japanned furniture, and its execution was rarely anything but the very finest quality. The same cannot be said of later papier-mâché which entered a definite decline during the 1870s following massive export orders, a saturation of the home market, and an increasing demand for genuine Chinese and Japanese goods at this period. Following the popularity of floral painting one further important stage in the decoration of papier-mâché occurred in 1864 when a patent for the application of powdered aluminium was obtained by Jennens and Bettridge. This gave an added wispiness to the views of romantic historical scenery so popular at this time, but heralded disfavour of the medium.

Another branch of the papier-mâché industry was the production of decoration suitable for ceiling and wall enrichments and picture and mirror frames by a method known as *carton pierre*. This was a French process much improved in England by an important firm of house decorators and furnishers, George Jackson and Sons. The material was pulped paper mixed with glue and whiting, which was then pressed into moulds and dried in a steady heat. In appearance it is often difficult to distinguish from carved wood, requiring the test of careful piercing with a needle or pin. The softer and more desirable carved wood will permit the insertion of the sharp point, the harder and cheaper *carton pierre* will not.

Cast iron

Cast iron was another improved material favoured by the Victorians for the manufacture of certain types of furniture. Although wrought iron had been used occasionally for chair frames for several centuries it was not until the mid nineteenth century that the full potential of the metal was realised. The most common examples of cast iron furniture still found today are those made for the garden or conservatory (see plate 136). These were cast to represent tree roots, trunks, and branches as well as complicated vines, ferns and formalised flowers. This pattern dates from the mid 1840s and is reflected in other fields of the applied arts, particularly contemporary silverware. Wrought iron became extremely popular in the construction of bed frames as well as for the newly fashionable rocking-chair and the other traditional garden and conservatory furniture, remaining with cast iron pieces very much in vogue until well into the 1880s.

Another pattern extremely popular for cast iron furniture was the 'Gothic' style so strongly advocated by A. W. Pugin. The tracery of Early English and Perpendicular windows, crocketed spires and flying buttresses could be faithfully produced in this medium and has proved a popular style for present-day copyists. Modern reproductions are usually of aluminium and while being lighter in weight and rust-proof, are easily recognisable from the original through the lack of finish at the edges of the mould joins.

THE ARTS AND CRAFTS MOVEMENT

The increasing bulkiness of furniture for the masculine apartments of the house during the William IV period and the early years of Victoria, the designs for which centred around the bastardised classical in the 'Etruscan' form, well-figured mahogany being the main timber used, was followed by the steady takeover in demand for furniture made in the 'Old French' style. Expanding from its primary function in the furnishing of female apartments into parlours, drawing-rooms, sitting-rooms and eventually dining-rooms, the style became one of the mainstays of furniture production and is essentially typical of the Victorian period. During the 1840s the Gothic designs of Augustus Welby Pugin became another mainstay; an example can be seen in plate 91. Like the 'Old French' it never quite faded from demand and underwent several revivals using different materials around the basic theme. One of these came during the 1860s with the use of ebonised wood lightened by low relief carving decorated with gold. A desk made in this manner by Messrs. Holland and Son can be seen in plate 119. This type of decoration rapidly became popular for other styles and a classical-pattern tripod table bearing evidence of this can be seen in plate 118.

The Warwick School of Carving

Following the inevitable influences on design of many of the countries represented at exhibitions, it is not surprising that the ensuing years became even more complicated in regard to the variety of designs, materials and methods of production available. Throughout the history of English furniture it can be seen that whenever there is an overriding demand or fashion for one style there eventually occurs a minority, in varying degrees of strength, in total opposition. During the 1850s we had the first real evidence of a revolt against the impending total use of machinery, and a movement which was to take many forms during the next sixty years was begun, almost unwittingly, by the Warwick School of Carving; oak as a suitable timber for fine furniture was to have a powerful revival.

At this time the ancient town of Warwick established itself as one of the important provincial sources of fine furniture with particular accent on carved decoration. The patterns were so elaborate as to be easily distinguishable from those of similar style produced in other areas, notably London and Newcastle, and were thus recognised and catalogued as being carving of the Warwick School. Such decoration was usually applied to large sideboards, buffets, cupboards, overmantle mirror frames and other ponderous wall pieces, and the range of subject matter knew no boundaries, with allegorical episodes from the age of chivalry depicted within borders of combined

Baroque, Rococo and Classical motifs. The one immediately recognisable feature peculiar to the carving of this period is the lack of sensitivity to proportion so apparent in previous ages. A combination of such unnatural partners as Rococo, Gothic and Chinoiserie in the mid eighteenth century succeeded in as much as simulated pagoda tops, figures, fences and festoons, cluster columns and pierced brackets all had continuity of scale. Such success cannot be accorded to the mid nineteenth-century carving wherein the decorative motifs of figures, frames, galleries and cornices give the appearance of having been made originally for a selection of different pieces of furniture, their scale being so out of context. The style, however, is definitely peculiar to the period and, for its fine execution, noteworthy if not universally considered praiseworthy, and its hand-made production set the scene for the continuation of such a movement in the ensuing decades.

William Morris

Working on the more secular aspects of the medieval or Gothic forms as opposed to the ecclesiastical and Elizabethan styles so popular during the 1840s was another designer whose name is now generally associated with the later Art Nouveau movement—William Morris. As early as the 1860s Morris established for himself a reputation of being a strict medievalist with strong beliefs in the eventual self-destruction of good taste and craftsmanship in the furniture trade through over-use of machinery and mass production. While the motives of William Morris and his followers were admirable it may be said with hindsight that they failed to see the intrusion of machinery in a constructive light. They stated categorically that good-quality furniture needed none of the elaborate decoration currently being applied to it, and more care and time should be taken over faultless construction, with each joint being so precisely cut as to obviate the need for glue. Unfortunately it had become evident by the 1860s that machine production was cheaper than individual manual production and that time was the costliest factor in an expanding industry. Thus the majority of the early furniture made to the directions of the Morris movement proved too plain to attract any very great attention from the wealthier furniture buyers and far too expensive for the average family.

By 1865 William Morris's firm, Morris & Co. (formerly Morris, Marshall, Faulkner & Co., established in 1861), felt gathering strength in the slow rise of interest in their type of medieval productions. The name of the style, Modern English Gothic or Early English, was intended to create an image of

Fig. 74 (left) and 75: Two nursery or 'child's chairs', examples of which can be found of varying degrees of quality dating from the seventeenth century. The type shown in fig. 75 is detachable from the base which then forms a companion table and is rare before the late eighteenth century.

purity and simplicity, with pegged joints and unpolished surfaces, and was strongly favoured by Charles Lock Eastlake in his publication *Hints on Household Taste,* published 1868. Like many other great men connected with the history of the furniture trade William Morris cannot as yet be held directly responsible for the creation of any specific piece, and it is his firm's chief furniture designer, the architect Philip Webb, who must be acknowledged as the prime mover in the manufacture of pieces to the patterns so favoured by Morris and popularised by Eastlake.

In 1860 Richard Charles produced the *Cabinet Makers' Monthly Journal of Design,* a publication which strongly favoured the Early English style, and in 1867 Bruce Talbert, a Glasgow trained architect and designer, published *Gothic Forms Applied to Furniture.* The next phase in the decoration of the Early English style was largely pioneered by the architect William Burges. During the 1860s Burges was working on the reconstruction of Cardiff Castle for the Marquess of Bute, and his designs for the interiors included painted furniture. While the furniture designed by Burges cannot be said to have greatly influenced the furniture industry in general, there must be considerable connection between his fondness of painted surfaces and the much admired Medieval-style pieces decorated by the artist Edward Burne-Jones, an example of which was shown at the International Exhibition in London, 1862.

It is evident from the appearance of much of the purist furniture of this period that what is now commonly associated with the term 'Art Nouveau' had its structural beginnings much earlier than generally realised. The name 'Art Nouveau' was not used to describe a particular style in this context until the turn of the century, but the combination of many of the essential ingredients which became so popular after 1880 was already clearly visible before the end of the 1860s. However, it was during this period that Charles Eastlake referred to such furniture as 'Art Furniture', striking a distinction between mass-produced and individually produced pieces. During the last thirty years of the nineteenth century the word 'Art' is found to appear with increasing regularity in newspapers and journals as a prefix to 'Furniture', 'Wallpaper' and 'Decoration', to such an extent that any new product, even from the cheapest manufacturers, was given this title to secure attention in an increasingly competitive market. But instead of killing the sale of all art designs, however well and expensively made, as happened with the over-production and over-sell of papier-mâché, enthusiasm increased until demand was such that the development of Art Nouveau was a fairly rapid one from individual to mass production by 1910.

Wallpaper design

During the last forty years of the nineteenth century a new visible link between designs for all household fittings and decoration emerged. Again it is possible to trace the origins of this to the creators of the Gothic, Medieval and Early English revival movements in general, with considerable influence from the designs of A. W. Pugin and William Morris in particular. The link was in the parity on an unprecedented scale of furniture decoration and wallpaper. The geometric Gothic designs for wallpaper by Pugin in 1843 perfectly complement his accompanying themes for furniture and fitments, as can be seen from his designs for the Houses of Parliament; and the sinuous, formalised foliate patterns of William Morris, first shown by him for wallpaper in the 'Daisy' pattern in 1862, were so often repeated on borders, mouldings and cornices, as well as in the shapes of metal mounts on furniture made to his designs. Morris went on to produce a series of wallpaper designs including the now famous 'Pomegranate', 'Trellis' and

'Acanthus' patterns, following which wallpaper gained great popularity among designers as a medium for the portrayal of their ideas.

The art of wallpaper design was to become an integral part of the Arts and Crafts Movement and a most important aspect of Art Nouveau. In this field the predominance of the heart shape so strongly advocated by C. F. Voysey, the sombre colours and curves of C. R. Mackintosh, and the popular long-stalked tulip caught in mid-movement created the backgrounds for many flowing-haired melancholy nymphs, and formed the the basis for designs executed in almost every medium, including glassware from the workshops of Emille Galle and Nancy and the translucent coloured work so effectively used for Tiffany lampshades.

The various facets of Art Nouveau have and will continue to have their origins traced further and further back in history, from early Chinese, Byzantine, even to Aztec sources, but English wallpaper designs can be definitely related for their inspiration in patterns and colours to the earlier Gothic tapestries.

The oldest block-printed wallpaper known in England covers the beams of the dining-room, entrance hall and ceiling of Christ's College, Cambridge, and dates from the early 1500s. The design is similar to that of contemporary brocades, but it was not until the late seventeenth century that a repeating pattern was introduced. Scenic panels on wallpaper appeared during the eighteenth century, and flock wallpaper, which was first recorded in the 1620s, became popular. All the major European developments in this industry seem to have taken place in France, but 'European' is specified because of the import and inevitable influence of Chinese wallpaper. This had been brought into western Europe since the booming export of Oriental wares through the various East India companies that were formed by the major countries in the West during the late sixteenth and early seventeenth centuries. The first examples of Chinese wallpaper appeared as gifts from grateful merchants (*Hongs*) to important customers, but their delicately painted scenes of exotic birds and flowers quickly created great demand, and a thriving industry in hand-painted rolls of wall-covering grew rapidly. As the concept of western Chinoiserie changed during its second great period in the mid eighteenth century, so too did the essential designs of Chinese wallpaper; for after the 1750s landscapes with figures became the more popular theme.

Unfortunately the artistic approach to wallpaper design was superseded eventually by commercialism for all but the wealthiest families, and by 1900 much of what was produced showed little thought or taste in its production. Also there was bound to be a reaction against the generally overdecorated appearance of the late Victorian home, and a fairly rapid decline in the demand for wallpaper occurred during the early twentieth century. It was replaced by a vogue for paint of a stone or putty colour, relieved only by the panelled effect created by picture rails and door frames.

THE REVIVAL OF OLD STYLES

International exhibitions

Another aspect to have considerable effect on the growth of the furniture industry was the increasing number of international and national exhibitions following the popularity of the Great Exhibition in 1851. There were exhibitions in Paris (1855), London (1862), Paris (1867), London (1871), and Paris (1878), after which the regularity was broken as other nations entered the field. Vienna in 1873 and Philadelphia in 1876 were the first two important occasions, with Australia joining in with Sydney and Melbourne in 1879 and 1880. In 1889 the Eiffel Tower was built for the exhibition in Paris that year, and a further exhibition was held in Paris in 1900. This followed the largest previous trade fair, at Chicago in 1893, and covered a greater area and had a larger attendance than any other exhibition of the nineteenth century. A Franco-British exhibition was held in London in 1908, and the last to come within the period of this text was held in Brussels in 1910. Unfortunately a fire caused considerable damage to the important buildings at this exhibition, resulting in a financial loss. During the last fifteen years of the nineteenth century several newly formed guilds and societies favouring the ideals of the William Morris movement joined forces to create the Arts and Crafts Exhibition Society and in 1888 held the first of three annual exhibitions. After a short break, another exhibition was held in 1893 followed by two more in 1896 and 1899. This then was the situation of a fashionable minority group with enthusiasm for artistic and creative craftsmanship; but for the student of Victorian furniture in more general terms many other aspects must be taken into consideration.

One of the most useful and often amusing sources of information concerning the background of the industry can be a periodical magazine or a directory as shown in plates 85 and 88. Here it is possible to find advertisements for a vast

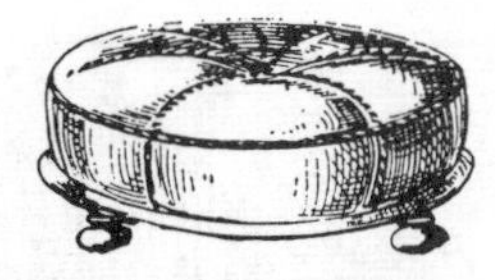
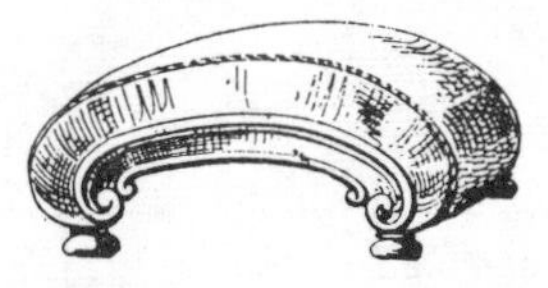

Fig. 76: Two foot stools showing the wide range of patterns available at the same time during the mid and late Victorian period. Show-wood frames of carved rosewood or walnut were popular when polished, while gilding and ebonised finishes were used on cheaper woods.

range of products, many of which have long since ceased to exist. Furthermore, because of an increasing amount of research and interest in this period, many of the more important contemporary publications are now being reprinted, many in a less voluminous form, and most at a more modest price than the original would now cost.

Any piece of furniture bearing a contemporary label pertaining to its origin is considerably more interesting from the historic viewpoint. Sadly, the practice of signing, stamping or labelling furniture was less popular in England than in France until the nineteenth century when, during the 1820s, more and more of the leading manufacturers and retailers took up this display of pride in their merchandise.

The refashioning of old furniture

With the comparatively sudden popularity of large-scale exhibitions, there was obviously a great demand on the majority of fine furniture makers and vendors to provide pieces, elaborate and exaggerated, intended more for display than for utility—display for showing their skills as much as for showing the wealth of the eventual purchaser; even so the majority of what may be considered typical Victorian furniture was made to a good standard and with some semblance of order in its decoration. But the cabinet-makers working to current designs with new materials were not the only source of supply, for, following the interest in the antique, many such craftsmen were commissioned to refashion old furniture, and in this respect the last thirty-five years of the nineteenth century may be recognised as the great age of the furniture pastiche.

As well as the numerous shops in London specialising in the sale of early oak pieces and parts, considerable responsibility for the large amounts of mutilated sixteenth and seventeenth-century oak items must rest on the larger house-

Fig. 77: A full-tester bed of the 1850-1875 period. The drawing shows an option in choice of bed-post below the complete canopy.

holds throughout the country wherein pieces handed down from generation to generation were thought to be ideal material for 'improvement' and alteration. Modernisation was in fact what they were doing, for pieces were actually over-carved in the Warwick School pseudo-Grinling Gibbons manner, and taken apart and reconstructed to make pieces of furniture suitable for houses of proportions different to those of earlier ages. The carved and turned supports for buffets, the deeply carved uprights and cross-members of panelled furniture, bedposts complete or in sections, cornice rails and other mouldings were the most popular parts of early oak furniture to be used in this way.

The frequent inclusion of leaded glazed door panels, sometimes with stained glass, later carving and new timber, are often sufficiently obvious factors to make the piece easily distinguishable from anything made in the sixteenth or seventeenth centuries. Of these three 'points to look for' the new timber is the least reliable, for when such alteration had been completed the whole article was either stripped and polished to a light honey colour, or heavily stained to a dark brown; the wear to edges and borders which for the first twenty or so years will show a clean bright colour has, by the 1970s, received enough further wear, exposure and polishing to make the contrast less distinct. If, after consideration of these points, there is still some doubt as to the authenticity of an article, the alteration in size and thus proportion may well be the

70 and 71. A bedroom table (above left) and companion washstand (above right) in finely figured mahogany by Gillow & Co. This type of heavy turned and tapering leg below formal box-top tables, with much use of reeding and cock bead edges, is typical of the 1825-1840 period and of the work of Gillow when constructed with the finest quality timbers, in the choice of which they were renowned.

72. (Left) A late 19th century butler's tray on folding stand; such pieces date from the last half of the 18th century, early examples being usually oval in shape, the edges of the oval hinged to form a galleried rectangle when in use. The butler's tray was produced in enormous quantities throughout the 19th century in all shapes and designs. This one can be definitely dated during the 1870-1890 period by the decoration of the stand.

73. (Above) A fine example of mid 19th century buhl work: the background of red tortoiseshell, ebony and gilt metal tracery; panels of buhl to the front edges of the legs, the top, and the four friezes of the table, enabling it to be used as a centre table when open. Finely cast mask heads, figures and scrolls are applied to the frame, knees and feet (c. 1855).

74. (Below) The card table open showing the end frieze and the deeply banded top with complementary border of buhl.

75. (Above) A fine mid-Victorian folding-top work and games table, the end columns and centre-turned stretcher with bead decoration, combined with a French scroll leg and porcelain castor. Such combination is peculiar to Victorian design. The top drawer and work box are decorated with well-figured walnut veneer and boxwood marquetry.

76. (Below) The table showing the top swivelled and opened — the two surfaces having parquetry inlay to form checker board, backgammon and cribbage or domino score board.

77. *(Above) A William IV period mahogany-frame reclining chair. The deeply shaped scroll arm supports are executed in the typical late Regency style. The tapering front legs are octagonal, a feature which became popular during this period. Unlike Minter's chair (plate 84) the degree of rake to the back of this chair is controlled by ratchets under each arm. The chair is stamped with the maker's name and bears his label with instructions for use on the underframe of the seat.* 78. *(Right) The stamp of 'R. Daws' and patent under 'G.R.' and crown.* 79. *(Below) The maker's label on the seat rail of the chair with instructions for its adjustment, printed in January 1834.*

Manner of using R. DAWS's Recumbent Easy Chair.

A person, while sitting in the Chair, may fix the back to any inclination, by raising the spring beneath that part each arm where the hand rests, and, while holding up both springs, press or draw the arms backward or forward the desired situation; and having loosed both springs at the same time, the back of the Chair will be found perfect safe to recline against. The back may also be raised from behind without touching the springs, or by a person at ea side, the dress having been first removed out of the way of the motion of the elbows.

The Leg Rests, which draw out in front, are finished variously, but generally for the stuffed pannel to be raised of the frame on a horse at the back end.

Respecting the permanence of the principle of this Chair, but little need be said, since R. DAWS is willing to ma OATH that the least derangement has not to his knowledge averaged one in FIVE HUNDRED during SEVEN years.

January 1834.—— *Robert Daws,* 17, *Margaret Street, Cavendish Square, London.*

80. (Left) A rosewood frame prie-dieu or praying chair, the back in openwork Gothic style (c. 1850).

81. (Above) A mid-Victorian rosewood prie-dieu chair with original needlework upholstery. This type of chair became popular during the early 1840s and remained so for the rest of the century.

82. (Left) The label on the underside of the seat rail of the prie-dieu, made by Oudin of Marseille.

83. *(Below) The maker's stamp on the chair (right), of 'G. Minter, Gerrard Street, Soho', the patent number, 'W.R.' with crown.*

84. *(Above right) An upholstered library chair c. 1830-1837. Plainly visible is the deeply carved formal foliate motif to the scroll-shape front of the arms over the much formalised leaf capping to the turned front legs. The lower front rail of this chair pulls forward to form a foot rest and the back reclines to an angle of 45 degrees under gentle pressure. Both front legs bear the maker's stamp.*

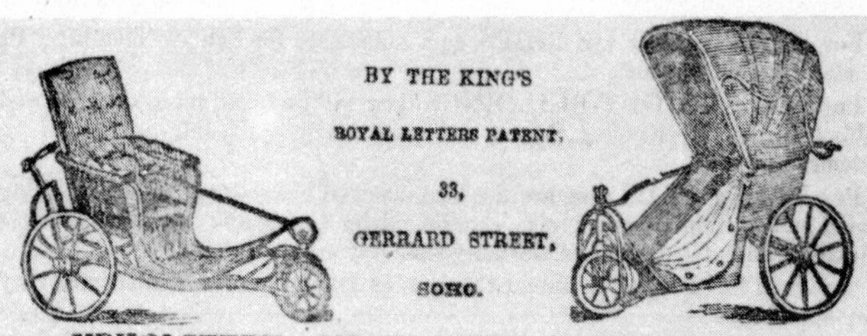

85. *(Above) The advertisement for G. Minter's patent 'self-acting reclining chair' as shown in plate 84.*

86 and 87. (Top and centre left) A portable water closet made by Robert Wiss, c. 1835. The mahogany case has the late Classical style panel columns surmounted by scallop shells. The door panels have the tops in low Gothic arch form, a most popular style for doors from 1830-1870. The hinged lid encloses a finely transfer-decorated blue and white porcelain bowl, which has a weighted trapdoor at the base. Half of the left side of the cupboard compartment is occupied by a zinc-lined water tank. A pumping action on the handle flushed the bowl.

Appendix.

Patent Portable & Fixed Water Closets.

ROBERT WISS invites an inspection of his New Method of Fixing WATER CLOSETS, by which contrivance the whole Apparatus is contained under the Seat. They are sent out ready for fixing, and all expence of Cisterns over head and Carpenters' Work is saved. They can be placed in any room, and made to imitate an article of Furniture.

CAUTION.

In consequence of unprincipled imitators having copied WISS'S (late Hawkins and Wiss) various Patent Water Closets, and advertised them as New and Improved, ROBERT WISS, the actual Inventor, very respectfully cautions the Public against the same, and begs to acquaint them that during the last Twelve Years, all the real Improvements have been effected by R. W. himself.

88. (Bottom left) An advertisement of Robert Wiss for his patent portable water closet, as shown in plates 86 and 87.

89. A fine quality rosewood circular top 'loo' table on quatrefoil base and carved vase-shaped pedestal. This type is popular today for use as a dining table in a modern home. The top can be tilted when not in use to stand against a wall (c. 1835).

90. The underside of the table shown in plate 89 has a mark of exceptional quality: the underneath has been painted to simulate the well-figured rosewood veneer of the top.

91. An oak and bronze book-carrier in the Gothic style showing considerable influence in the crocketed corner pilasters of the architectural designs by Augustus Welby Pugin (c. 1850).

92. A rosewood-frame upholstered chair showing the French influence so popular during the early Victorian period. Often bought en suite with a matching armchair and settee.

93. (Above) A fine early Victorian rosewood 'loo' table, the Baroque-style centre pedestal and tripod base deeply carved. Each panel of the lower base, the block and top bear the registered patent mark for the year 1849.

94. (Below left) The centre panel of the lower part of the base showing the stamped patent mark, used as an integral part of the design. 95. (Below right) The underside of the table (plate 93), showing the rails or runners secured to the top by screws and the holes covered with dome turned discs. This was a 19th-century practice; such holes on 18th century furniture were usually filled and planed flat.

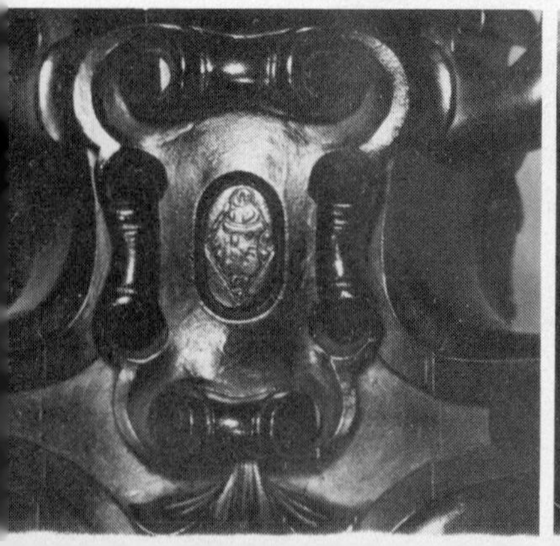

96. (Above left) A rosewood writing desk with one long drawer below the writing surface. The heavy nulling to the borders remained popular for many years after its introduction during the late 1820s. The pierced framework to the gallery and end supports became popular during the 1840s, and illustrations for similar desks can be seen in the catalogues of the Great Exhibition of 1851. 97. (Above right) A walnut Canterbury/whatnot. The inverted cup shape at the lower part of the column is similar to that introduced during the late 17th century, but not until the mid 19th century did this feature have the surface carving with a bell motif. The top front edge of the drawer is stamped 'Gillow'. 98. (Right) A mahogany and walnut veneered corner whatnot, the graduating shelves supported with barley sugar twist turned columns; the openwork top gallery and friezes to the shelves are typical of the work produced after 1847, reaching a zenith during the mid 1850s.

99. (Left) An early Victorian chiffonier of well-figured mahogany (c. 1845). The pointed Gothic arch doors combine with pseudo-medieval carving in the corners below double-scroll shelf supports. All of these features became popular during the early Victorian period. 100. (Below left) A mid-Victorian music Canterbury of fine quality showing much influence in the Baroque (Old French) style on the carved outer partition (c. 1845). 101. (Below right) A fine example of the intricate patterns achieved by the manufacturers of 19th century buhl decoration. This casket, which contained personal stationery, was one of a pair; the other, with reverse brass to tortoise-shell decoration, contained perfume bottles. (10 inches long, c. 1845.)

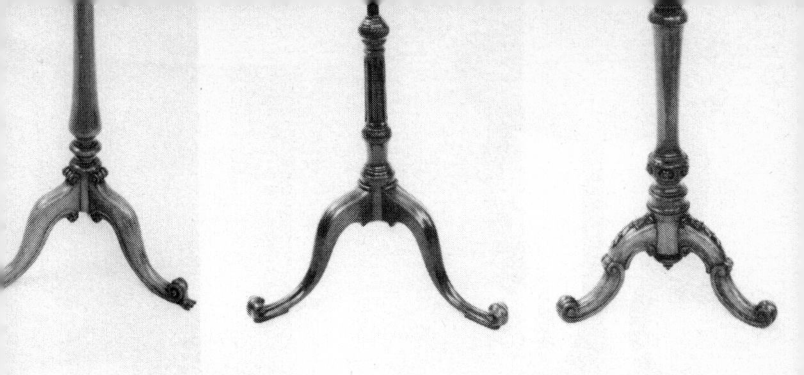

102, 103 and 104. (Above left to right) Three tripod bases. Plate 102 is a 19th century interpretation of a 'French Hepplewhite' period tripod base (c. 1765). 103. The immediate recognition of one from the other is made possible by the proportions of the legs, the wider splay being earlier. 104 shows the legs formed of double 'C' scrolls of the 19th century Baroque style with bell husk carving to the knees from the English Adam style: such a combination indicates Victorian manufacture.

105. (Below left) An Admiral Fitzroy barometer (c. 1870). This type of barometer was first produced in 1860, and included a sealed storm glass, the contents of which were kept secret by Admiral Fitzroy. There are also instructions for making forecasts from natural observations. 106. (Below centre) A William IV period rosewood pole screen. The banner is adjustable in height by means of a circular lead weight, seen here below the frame. The screen is a panel of Berlin needlework in the Chinese taste on an ivory ground, which helps confirm the early date. After the late 1840s a black background for such needlework was more popular. 107. (Below right) A mid 19th century rosewood pole screen on carved tripod base in the French style. The banner is a panel of Berlin needlework in the historical romantic taste (c. 1850), with a dark background to the border.

108. (Above left) A fine quality rosewood and marble top occasional table (c. 1830). Although the 'C' scroll supports are of the finest shape the small brackets at the joints and the triform platform base make this 19th rather than 18th century. The timber and carving are of the finest quality.

109. (Above right) One of a pair of rosewood and gilt corner tables with marble top and base. The back frame would originally have had a mirror panel. The heavy scrolling support is typical of the William IV period interpretation of the Old French (c. 1830).

110. An unusual example of Tunbridge ware, an octagonal basket with laminated swing handle. Accurate dating of Tunbridge ware can be difficult as it was produced in much the same way following the advent of machine cutting veneer. However, the bouquet of flowers here seen on a light ground would suggest c. 1860 rather than later.

111. (Above) A papier-mache writing box, the lid decorated with fine gilt drawing around an asymmetrical bordered landscape in the romantic taste (c. 1840).

112. (Below) A papier-mache portable writing desk or lap-desk with gilt and bright enamel borders around a central bouquet of flowers to the folding lid. Between 1840 and 1870 the variety of decorative materials increased and the quality declined. The painting of flowers and application of gilt to this box and the construction of its interior are of the very highest quality (c. 1845).

113. (Above left) A child's piano stool, the heavy mahogany base machine-carved with scrolling patterns below the adjustable seat (c. 1865).

114. (Above right) An oak music seat (c. 1885). The primitive Gothic style apparent in the curved legs was popular from c. 1870 to c. 1895.

115. (Below left) One of a pair of display cabinets in the French taste (c. 1850). The front and top are veneered with kingwood and rosewood crossbanding and gilt metal mounts. The open shaped ends were popular on such cabinets c. 1845-1880.

116. (Below right) An early Victorian spinet stool, the upper part of the column with the formalised lotus motif which remained popular from c. 1830-1860. The seat height is not adjustable and retains its original upholstery (c. 1840).

117. (Left) An early Victorian cabinet with marble top, open ends and enclosed centre cupboard. The veneer is golden-colour maple with gilt enrichments of gesso and ormolu. Panels to the doors are porcelain and signed on the reverse 'Copeland and Garrett' with their mark for the period of 1833-47.

118. (Right) A tripod-base circular-top table of ebonised and gilt wood in the Classical style of the period after 1860. The top is pine with a plush velvet cover.

119. (Below) A partner's desk of ebonised and gilt wood with parquetry-inlaid decoration in the Gothic style, the top edge of the drawer fronts and doors stamped 'Holland and Son' (c. 1860).

120. (Above left) A fine dining chair of the late Regency period: the overhanging top rail panelled between realistically carved foliate decoration above Classical style centre splat; curved sabre legs (c. 1830). 121. (Above centre) A mahogany arm or carving chair of the late Regency period: the foliate carved back splat and overhanging back rail above simply moulded legs and scroll arms (c. 1830). 122. (Above right) A William IV period rosewood mahogany dining chair.

123. (Below left) A lyre-shape scroll-back parlour chair of mahogany, the seat of deep buttoned velvet upholstery (c. 1845). 124. (Below centre) A parlour chair of golden-colour maple with finely curved lines and excellent proportions (c. 1845). 125. (Below right) A parlour or dining chair of solid rosewood (c. 1850).

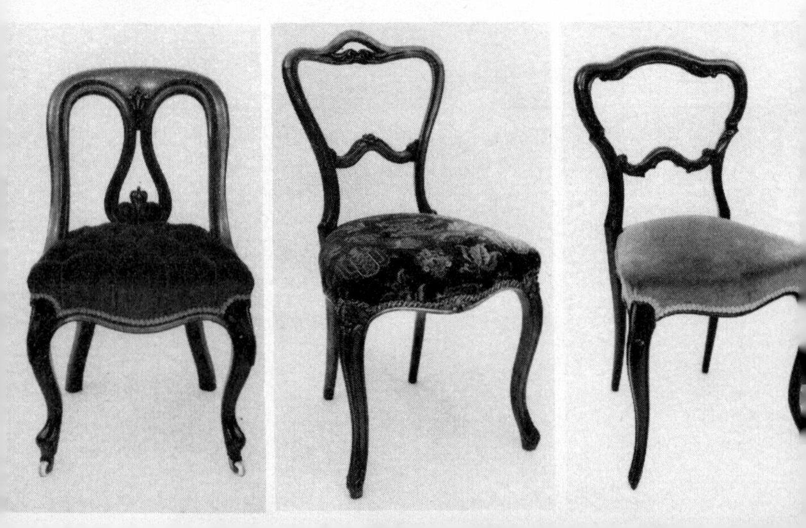

126. (Above left) A rosewood parlour or dining chair of the mid-Victorian period. Examples of this type can be found dating from the mid 1830s till well into the 1860s. 127. (Above right) Rocking chair — probably by Messrs Thonet of Vienna (c. 1855). Bentwood furniture introduced to England by Messrs Thonet in the 1830s became extremely popular during the Victorian period. The finest examples are ebonised with a gloss finish, as illustrated here, or painted in simulation of superior timbers. By the end of the 19th century overproduction had caused bentwood furniture to fall from a place in high fashion but its production continued to be enormous. 128. (Below left) The luxury version of the rocking chair, upholstered throughout and having a fine-quality maplewood frame. The front arm can be seen to sweep down into a continuous curve which forms the rocker. Many examples of upholstered rockers are made up from an upholstered chair being joined to two rockers. 129. (Below right) A late Regency rosewood early William IV upholstered armchair with similar formalised foliate capping to the front edges as shown in the reclining chair (plate 84). Here the formalised leaf capping to the legs is seen elongated to produce a reeded effect (c. 1830).

131. (Above) A close-up of the seat rails of the chair showing the unplaned machine cut marks which give instant recognition of the late manufacture.

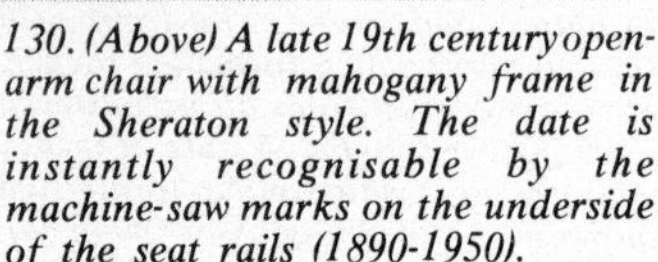

130. (Above) A late 19th century open-arm chair with mahogany frame in the Sheraton style. The date is instantly recognisable by the machine-saw marks on the underside of the seat rails (1890-1950).

132. (Right) A fine quality three-tier whatnot; the shelves and drawer front are decorated with finely figured burr walnut veneer with rosewood and boxwood stringing.

133. (Below) A close-up of the top edge of the drawer showing the clearly stamped makers' name 'Gillow & Company'.

134. (Left) A late 19th century mahogany open-arm chair in a style often referred to as 'Edwardian Sheraton'. The only similarity between this and the designs of Thomas Sheraton is the delicate appearance; otherwise the combination of curving front legs carved at the knees, deeply scrolling arms, ivory and boxwood stringing and marquetry, and a pierced and carved centre panel create an image peculiar to this late period.

135. (Below) The back panel of the chair, showing in detail the marquetry of boxwood and ivory over the pierced and carved centre splat. Also visible are the white streaks in the grain caused by the drying out of the grain-filler used in the late 19th and early 20th centuries prior to the application of French polish. Polish and grain-fillers are discussed in greater detail on pages 182 and 190.

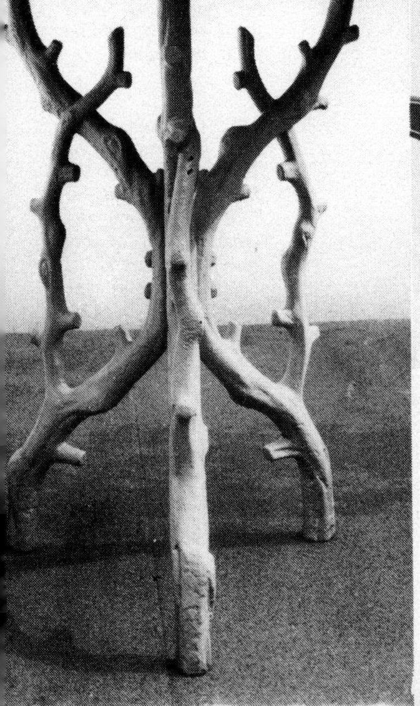

136. (Left) A cast iron table base in the rustic style.

137. (Top left) The underneath of the same drawer (see plates 132-133) — the fine quality and construction seen here is the type most desirable in Victorian furniture. The back fixing of the drawer bottom with three screws in cut slots is a 19th century idea. Many inferior quality pieces do not have such fixing and a common fault today is to find the drawer linings slipping out from the back.

138. (Centre left) The end of the drawer clearly showing the fine quality dovetails. Also to be noted is that all but the show-wood on this and any other good quality articles is of mahogany.

139. (Bottom left) The underneath of the whatnot with the drawer removed — here can be seen the 'clean' effect of the unexposed areas of wood and again the fineness of quality and materials.

140. (Left) An English or American copy of the Japanese table illustrated in plate 141; the construction and material used are both inferior, with coverings to shelf and top of woven rattan. This type of furniture was mass produced and examples are of interest only for comparison.

141. (Right) A fine bamboo table of the Japanese period (c. 1885) — the asymmetrical lower structure covered with embossed leather below lacquer panel top. Fine examples of this important period and fashion are rare.

142. (Left) An early Japanese period two-seat settee — the original cane seat covered in American cloth at a later date (c. 1870).

143. (Right) Small bracket clock in the Edwardian Sheraton style — apart from the obvious date ascertained from the movement and face of this clock, the unlikely combination of oval panel and stringing between quarter columns would point to either late manufacture or an 18th century piece improved at a later date. The quality of the stringing is in no way fine enough to compare with that of the 18th century.

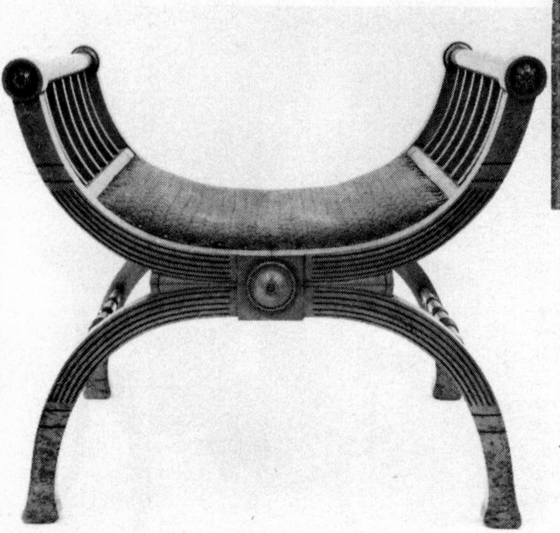

144. (Left) A fine dressing stool, the beechwood frame shaped and decorated with reeding in the late 19th century classic or Egyptian style; recognition of the date can be made from the reeding terminating in cross-bands, and the inclusion of flower-head paterae at the tops of the arms (c. 1890).

145. (Right) A set of oak book-shelves: the openwork sides and upper back pierced in the plain medieval style so favoured by the Arts and Crafts movement. The front to each sloping shelf bears a panel of planished copper embossed in low relief with typical Art Nouveau scrolling tendrils, heart and tulip-shape flowers (c. 1900).

most important single guide. Although it is generally assumed that during the Victorian period the greatest demand was for extravagantly large furniture, there was in fact an enormous demand for smaller pieces bearing the same amount of decoration as their larger counterparts. The reduction in dimensions, the almost too perfect 'squaring-up' of joints and an excessive amount of carving, certainly on a small cupboard or buffet, coupled with the features mentioned above, should lead to strong suspicion of nineteenth-century adaptation.

As the nineteenth century progressed and the twentieth century began, each of the major period styles of English furniture was reproduced. Following the popularity of oak and the Elizabethan, Gothic and Ecclesiastical styles, the Queen Anne style in an equally modified form and the use of walnut became extremely fashionable. Almost at the end of the century and during the first twenty-five years of the twentieth century this taste was joined by a vogue for furniture in the Chippendale style, with mahogany as the necessary timber. Also from *c.* 1895 throughout the next twenty years there was a demand for lighter, more delicate furniture which was supplied by the manufacture of what is today recognised, somewhat misleadingly, as Edwardian Sheraton; the woods most used for the production of this were naturally mahogany and satinwood, with considerable accent on the inlaying of a variety of contrasting coloured woods and other materials, such as ivory, mother-of-pearl, enamels and pewter. In each of these period revivals the use of modern production and materials and questionable improvements in proportion are usually sufficient evidence of their out-of-period origin.

Period revivals

The one disturbing factor during the later nineteenth century was the change in the reasons behind the alterations of authentic early pieces. There are in existence many examples of walnut furniture, dating from the beginning of the eighteenth century, which were altered in order to conform with the appearance of the most up-to-date Victorian 'Queen Anne' walnut reproductions. The alterations might have been structural, involving considerable cabinet work to reduce size, or the separation and modification of two-part chest furniture, or merely the removal of all old colour and patina to be replaced by layers of glossy varnish. However, by the time Chippendale-style furniture had become fashionable, considerable interest and demand for the genuine article had developed, and the more ordinary household items of the mid and late eighteenth century were no longer altered for innocent utility reasons, but were recarved and otherwise made to look finer purely for monetary gain on the part of unethical vendors. An interest in antiques had begun, and with it came the fakers (see page 180).

Of the many smaller but still unfortunate changes made in genuine attempts to improve rather than spoil during the nineteenth century, the most commonly seen today is the replacement of original metal handles with turned wooden knobs to the drawers of chests and tables, cabinets and commodes. Anything with a push-pull action was a potential subject for this regrettable practice. Finely turned knobs or pulls had appeared on fashionable furniture during the last quarter of the eighteenth century, and had remained a popular alternative to metal since that time. They were, however, much more an integral part of the overall design of the piece than the large bulbous mushroom-shaped knobs that came so much into vogue from the late 1830s. The earlier turned knobs were smaller in comparison and were fixed with a straight dowel glued into a fractionally undersize hole in the drawer front. Victorian knobs were attached by means of a screw-turned dowel fitting into a threaded hole in the drawer front, sometimes without glue.

Of the three revived styles that became so popular during the late Victorian and Edwardian periods, those of the Queen Anne walnut and Chippendale mahogany furniture were copied and faked for unethical sale to a far greater extent than the Sheraton style. Although a considerable amount of plain furniture dating from the last quarter of the eighteenth century was repolished and re-inlayed in the Sheraton manner, most of this was done as a legitimate 'improvement', for comparatively little value was attached to the antique or historic interest of such furniture at this time. Nearly all Victorian and Edwardian period repolishing is easily detectable by the hard glossy surface, aptly described by the trade term 'piano polish', over a distinctly stained surface—generally bright ginger for walnut and deep red for mahogany. However, cheaper timber was used for much of the plain provincial furniture of the late eighteenth century and so the repolisher had to use larger quantities of pre-polish grain filler to prepare the surface of this open-textured wood. When the old patina, consisting of a primary layer of spirit varnish followed by very many years of waxing and dusting, is removed, the raw surface of the wood is exposed. The more open the grain, the more air penetrates the wood. Thus when the surface is again sealed with a hard polish it is only a matter of time before minute air bubbles appear, further drying and shrinking the grain filler to give the effect of pale streaks, where in the original dark lines denote the grain. A fuller description of patina and the development of furniture polishes can be found on page 182.

Berlin embroidery

Plate 106 shows a rosewood-base pole-screen with a particularly fine panel of contemporary needlework for the banner. Such screens became extremely popular during the eighteenth century for both decorative and utility purposes. They were an ideal way of displaying panels of fine needlework, either bought at great expense from abroad or produced by the talented ladies of the household, while at the same time performing their essential function of screening the fierce heat of the fire from the faces of the delicate but often over-made-up women for whom it was unseemly to appear pink or flushed. Needlework continued to grow as a popular and rewarding pastime for all classes during the nineteenth century, considerably encouraged by the import of patterns originally produced in Berlin. The basic principal of the Berlin panel is that of squared paper printed with a pattern in colours, each square representing a stitch of needlework—similar to the basic principle of painting by numbers.

The first patterns were published in 1803 and the earliest records of their appearance in England are of 1805. To begin with, the cross or tent stitch was used, and the wool, which came from Gotha before being dyed in Berlin, was imported with the patterns. The firm of Wilks of Regent Street recognised the potential in this merchandise and by 1831 were retailing all the imported and home-produced materials and accessories for this embroidery: by 1840 there were some fourteen thousand different Berlin patterns available. It is from the contrasting colours and complexity of stitches that nineteenth-century needlework can be approximately dated, the most subdued and uniform being the earlier. Some of the finer examples of the William IV period were executed with silk instead of wool, and plate 106 shows an example of this with a Chinoiserie-theme panel mounted behind glass in an adjustable frame on a pole base. The background is cream, which with white was the most popular colour during the 1830s and 1840s. During the 1850s black was considered a more suitable background for the violent primary colours that had by then become fashionable. Unfortunately fast dyes were rarely used, and much of the original startling effect has been lost through fading. By the end of the 1850s, beads were also incorporated, and the deep pile effect of velvet was obtained

Fig. 78: A half-tester bed of the mid-Victorian period. The solid D-shape foot with free-standing turned columns is typical of the 1860-1890 period. The term 'half-tester' describes the overhanging half canopy as distinct from the 'full-tester' bed in fig. 77.

by the inclusion of chenille and making the stitches with long loops prior to cutting in low-relief shapes. From the middle of the century the most popular designs were floral, from single specimens to enormous intricate displays, and by this time the designs were also printed directly on to the canvases as an alternative to the paper patterns. As an essential part of the production of the Berlin patterns was the mechanical process of mass-printing, it is not surprising that the vogue was subject to considerable criticism from the founders and followers of the Arts and Crafts movement. Such criticism, both oral and written, increased towards the end of the century to a sufficient degree to have a noticeable influence on the rising standard of originality and quality in amateur and professionally made embroidery.

Tunbridge ware

Yet another form of surface decoration which reflected faithfully the changing phases in Victorian taste is a type of veneer known as Tunbridge ware. Originating in Tunbridge Wells, the work can be compared in appearance to mosaic, miniature parquetry or even fine needlework, but its construction is different to all three. Long faceted strips of contrasting coloured woods are glued and bound together until set in a single column. Great skill is needed in the arrangement of these thin strips for it is during this part of the operation that the desired picture is built up. When the column is dry, slices are cut from the end in the manner of veneer, and these can then be applied to the surface of the article to be decorated.

An example can be seen in plate 110. The earliest records of Tunbridge ware refer to wood turners in that district during the late sixteenth and early seventeenth centuries and give evidence that this was a popular method of making decorative turned wood bowls, cups and other small objects. The natural waters in the Tunbridge area were found to have a chemical reaction on some woods, in particular the local oak which attained a curious green. During the late seventeenth century, when various dyes and acids were often used to change the natural colours of woods, Tunbridge ware became much in demand; by the end of the eighteenth century all manner of small boxes had lids and sides decorated with panels of geometric or floral patterns. In the nineteenth century landscapes and fanciful castles, as well as realistic scenes of local importance, were produced in large numbers to supply the ever growing fashion for collecting souvenirs that was to become so much a part of Victorian life. In 1787 one correspondent wrote that in his opinion trade in Tunbridge ware would have improved had it first been exported and then introduced as a new 'foreign' merchandise, illustrating once again that the emphasis of demand was on novelty rather than quality. The development of fine cutting machinery benefited the manufacturers of Tunbridge ware and its production and popularity reached a zenith during the last half of the nineteenth century.

The collection of souvenirs at the slightest excuse began to have a visible effect on furniture during the late 1860s. About this time extra shelf space started to appear in any suitable area of cabinets, sideboards, dressers and other wall and chimney furniture. The sides of mirror frames were formed of tiers of small shelves, each supported on turned columns and often with pierced galleries around the lower edges and canopies at the top. This concept was adapted for overmantles and sideboard backs, and the inclusion of panes of mirror-glass to reflect the objects on display added to the apparently required sense of clutter. Graduated corner shelves, both hanging and free-standing, also became extremely popular, and an early example can be seen in plate 98. As with every other change in basic structure the side and corner shelves in straight or graduating form were made in every currently fashionable style and give a further indication of the vast range of style and quality available to the buying public during the last thirty years of the nineteenth century.

Bentwood furniture

Meanwhile two further imports had become established patterns to add to the complexity of this crowded period.

Fig. 79: A single-end day-bed or couch, the decoration of the show-wood frame displaying a combination of Baroque scrolls and formal classical gauged lines, on turned feet (after c. 1850).

Bentwood furniture became extremely popular during the last half of the nineteenth century following its initial introduction during the 1830s. Unfortunately, like so many successful Victorian ideas, bentwood furniture eventually became synonymous with the undesirable through cheapness and over-production, but during its heyday in the period mentioned some graceful examples were produced; the rocking chair illustrated in plate 127 is an example. Bentwood furniture was invented by the firm of Thonet in Vienna, and much of its popularity can be accounted for by the lightness and strength of the pieces, coupled with attractive curved shapes, the considerable comfort in the cane-seated chairs and moderate price. Messrs Thonet opened a showroom in London and through this sold enormous quantities to the English market. The wooden parts of the furniture were shaped in steam presses and were finished in a variety of ways, the most popular of which was ebonising or graining in simulation of more expensive timber. The production of bentwood furniture, particularly 'single' chairs, continued well into the twentieth century, by which time for reasons of economy the traditional cane seat had been superseded by the circular plywood seat machine-stamped in a variety of shallow relief patterns.

ORIENTAL STYLES AND ART NOUVEAU

The Japanese influence

A considerable demand for Oriental art of all forms has been apparent in the Western world since knowledge of its existence first filtered back through the early explorers, and certainly after the establishment of the European East India companies in the seventeenth century. Their trade was more with China however, since Japan remained persistently insular until the period of the Meiji or Enlightened Government, which began during the late 1860s. In 1867 the accession of the young Mitsuhito led to drastic changes in governmental policies, and the subsequent years saw a gradual lifting of many of the centuries-old barriers that had hitherto been Japan's tradition. Mitsuhito sent his brother to the International Exhibition in Paris and, although there was strong and powerful opposition, the possibilities of a world market were beginning to be realised. The government wisely assisted the production of goods saleable in the Western world and found an unexpected and eager demand for her culture and produce in England. Japanese was the one style that immediately captured the imaginations of aesthetes, historians, followers of the Arts and Crafts movement—both genuine and parasite, copyist manufacturers, and eventually a vast cross-section of the general public. In view of the controversial reception given to most of the showpieces made specially for exhibitions and the prestige of the manufacturers, and the limited sources of inspiration self-imposed by the Arts and Crafts movement, it is not surprising that the Japanese style found such immediate and universal favour. Examples of the style were first shown publicly at the second Great Exhibition in London in 1862 and by 1870 the Japanese taste had become a craze that was to affect design in one form or another for the next forty years. Among the chief exponents of the early style were Burges, Godwin, Dresser, Whistler, Leach and the delightfully named Lafcadio Hearn whose writings were extremely successful. Authentic and pseudo Japanese goods were first sold in London by Messrs Farmer and Rogers, and the firm of Liberty. The style had a tranquil quality, a simplicity of form, and an inherent beauty which conveyed something of the timeless Japanese culture; it caught the imagination as well as the eye, conjuring up pictures of a far-off Utopia brought within the reach of every front-room and parlour in England. It was during this period that the masses of fans, sun-shades, scrolls and screens, lacquer boxes, ivory carvings, exotic gowns and small items of furniture first started to spread throughout the home market. The coats, shawls, kimonos and other embroidered silks were machine-made, but were of sufficiently exquisite quality to lead to the popular present-day belief that they were of a much earlier date and hand-made.

The already well-organised commercial import of Japanese

wares was further supplemented by the individual tourist visiting the Orient. From the large amounts of such merchandise still resting in English homes it can be assumed that every passenger and crew member of the ships that called in Japanese ports purchased at least one souvenir. Because the Japanese were so adept at producing their traditional patterns with the help of modern machinery, tourists had the added incentive to buy of the hope that their purchases might be of antique as well as decorative value. This is particularly true of all kinds of ornaments, and before the sale or acquisition of such pieces today an expert should be consulted.

The most popular type of Japanese furniture encountered now is that made of bamboo. The asymmetrical designs often incorporated one or several panels of lacquer, with shelves formed of woven rattan cane, sometimes covered with embossed leather. An example of a Japanese table can be seen in plate 141.

It was not long before English manufacturers started to use natural and simulated cane as a decorative feature, and by the 1890s a cheap copy of the original was available for the mass market (plate 140). As had happened several times before, the over-production of a particular style or material inevitably killed the fashionable demand, and by 1900 Japanese furniture was beginning to lose its place in high fashion. The accompanying decorative objects, however, remained as a standard part of design in varying degrees for many years.

Art Nouveau

Being considerably inspired by Japanese motifs, the Arts and Crafts movement continued to flourish, developing into what has become one of the best-known art forms of the nineteenth century—Art Nouveau. The name was taken from L'Art Nouveau, the Paris shop of S. Bing whose first dealings were in imported Japanese wares. The style that emerged had an apparent ancestry too vast to be contemplated in a short text, but it also had an originality very much of its time. Arthur Lasenby Liberty, formerly manager of Messrs Farmer and Rogers who had dealt so successfully with the Japanese merchandise on exhibition in 1862, opened the existing world-famous shop in 1875, and the highly fashionable textiles and ornaments that he sold were known in some quarters as 'Style Liberty'. This term originated in Italy, one of the best-informed European countries, which continued to import rather than contribute to the creation of Art Nouveau. The most immediately recognisable forms of weightless, undulating components in any early Art Nouveau decoration can be traced back to the

Fig. 80: A four-seat centre ottoman, the typical buttoned seat and back supported by four turned legs and castors (c. 1860, but the dating of fig. 70 should be taken into consideration with all such pieces).

painter and poet William Blake, but even closer examination of his work at the beginning of the nineteenth century can lead the enthusiast to delve still further into the history of art to find the origins of this style.

The heavy Gothicism of William Morris was lightened, the abandonment of Aubrey Beardsley was controlled, and the stark vertical lines of Christopher Dresser, Godwin and even Mackmurdo were eased in an attempt to appeal to a wider market for the mass-produced furniture industry. Strangely enough it was the bleakness of the unbending vertical lines so strongly advocated by these men, again considerably influenced by Japanese architecture, which remained into the twentieth century to form the basis for the clear-cut designs of the 'functional' style.

However, the bulk, and therefore what must be considered most typical, of the furniture manufactured during the first ten years of the twentieth century was in the antique or 'period' style. The growing interest in genuine antiques continued to influence the faker and improver, and the supply of spurious as well as cheap imitation antique furniture was plentiful. The fully upholstered three-piece suite became a popular 'front' room furnishing, and the market was further bolstered by the import of continental and American furniture. Of the latter, Japanese-style 'rattan' pieces and the rectangular box-frame chiming clocks with coloured glass panels to the doors are typical examples.

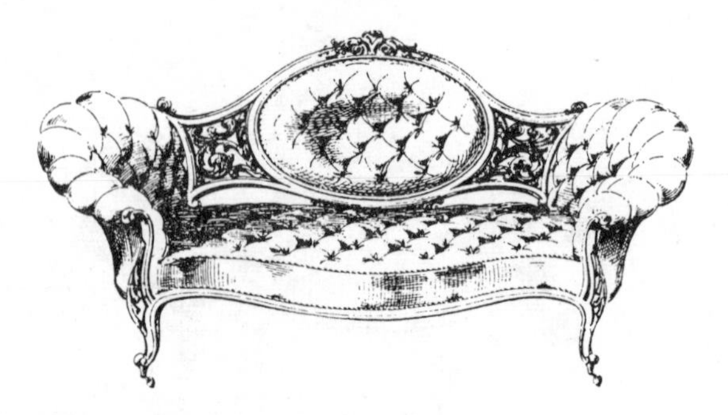

Fig. 81: An open-back settee in the Old French style with an oval panel to the back, between finely pierced and carved sections (after c. 1850).

Ambrose Heal

Viewing the situation from the present time one can see the need for a class of furniture to bridge the gap between the extremely expensive Art Nouveau style and the cheaper, plentiful 'period' styles. A pioneer of such furniture was Ambrose Heal who, as a trained cabinet-maker and member of a well-established family business in London, showed considerable foresight in his designs for bedroom and, later, general household items. The characteristics of his furniture were plain symmetrical lines showing much influence of the later Art Nouveau and Japanese styles, with an unpolished or 'weathered' oak as the most used timber. The designs were produced with commercial manufacture in mind, and by the early 1900s success in this field became apparent. Within a short time many of Heal's ideas were accepted as standard patterns for contemporary manufacturers in a variety of qualities. The more important and exhibition pieces were often decorated with inlay in traditional English manner, with chequered bands of various materials being a popular motif. The more ordinary pieces were essentially plain, any decoration taking the form of a moulded edge to drawer fronts in a simplified mid sixteenth-century style, or geometric patterns created by juxtaposition of timber grain—for example the very popular circle within a quartered square door panel. Drawer and door handles were of turned wood or sunken, the drawer front being pierced in an elongated oval or heart shape with sufficient undercut at the top for the fingers to secure a grip. Kitchen furniture—tables, rush-seated chairs, cupboards and dressers—had the appearance of elementary construction in the extreme, but the quality was, and still is, easily discernible. The choice and treatment of the timber and the precision with which the joints were cut are sufficient guides to establish the class of furniture being viewed. Japanese oak was used in favour of the European variety for it was found to have a much closer grain and possess medullary rays of much stronger contrasting colour than the former type of timber. Symmetrically designed furniture, with increasing severity in its functional appearance, grew steadily in demand through the 1920s and 1930s, equalling and gradually superseding the popularity of the period styles.

Fig. 82: A Sutherland table (c. 1860). Small and medium-size occasional tables of this pattern were very popular during the last half of the nineteenth century and were made to a variety of designs and quality. The extremely narrow top, in proportion to the long leaves, is the important feature of the Sutherland table.

Fig. 83: A shaped circular-top table, the edge with deep fringe over the bobbin-turned tripod base of 'cat' form. This type of support, where turned members screw into a central ball, may be found as holders for bowls and dishes and became extremely popular during the Victorian period.

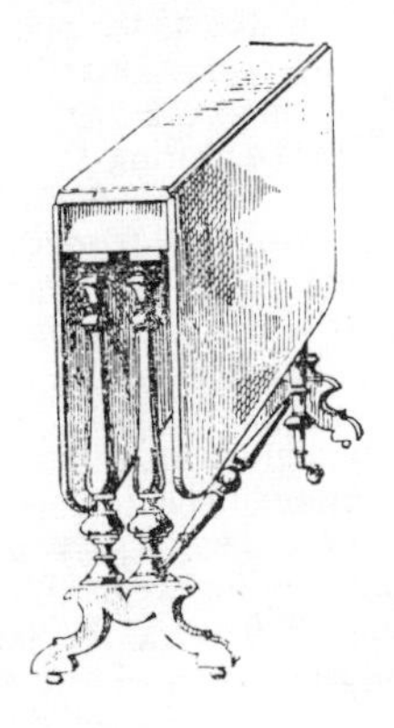

FAKES, ALTERATIONS, IMPROVEMENTS

The title of this chapter summarises the main types of spurious articles likely to be encountered today. An increase in demand for any merchandise inevitably leads at some point to the production of inferior facsimiles, and old English furniture is certainly no exception. This is no new situation. The work of carvers, cabinet makers and polishers of the early 1900s is a memorial to the enthusiastic but inexpert collectors and the unethical or ignorant vendors of that period. Therefore today we not only have to be aware of the skilled faker and reproducer of the present time but the work of such men since the turn of the century. To complicate matters even more there are the items brought up to date in appearance or altered in shape and use by enthusiastic amateurs during the late Victorian period. During the 1860s the Warwick School of Carving popularised a style of extremely high quality but over-elaborate carved decoration on furniture. This rapidly became a fashionable hobby for middle and upper class citizens in Victorian society who were undoubtedly responsible for the massacre of many fine pieces of early oak. But in an age of tremendous industrial development little respect was shown to ordinary household articles of a past era, and to recarve such items was a means of practice and therefore a justifiable improvement. However, their motives were at least honest if completely misguided. In contrast, during the early 1900s the services of the skilled faker were in demand to appease the appetites of wealthy collectors of the antique. Having obtained the finest known examples available, these men sought the unknown and the impossible. Furniture made to designs undreamt of by Kent, Chippendale and Hepplewhite was forced into famous collections through various channels by pitting the pride of one collector against another. Inevitably several law suits followed during the 1920s bringing disrepute to all concerned. But to be fair, few of the collectors and their advisers had dealings with bow-front chests, pot cupboards, washstands and the like. Not for them the utility article which is an important part if not the basis for a thorough knowledge of furniture and its construction.

The complete fake is an article made with old materials, in the old method of construction by a highly skilled craftsman and produced for the sole purpose of deception. The majority of fakes of this description were made during the early part of this century, and having had over fifty years genuine wear and tear their discovery can sometimes be difficult. But while the skilled fakers had a knowledge of the design and styles of the early periods, being naturally proud of their work, few resisted the temptation of incorporating a small feature somewhere on the article, almost like a trademark. This might be a minor addition or omission which would not have occurred on the genuine piece. A fact which may well have confused the original purchaser is that these fakes were fine articles which, had they been genuine, would have been treated with respect throughout their lifetime and therefore not expected to show signs of constant use. But once exposed as false, reverence ceased, and half a century of daily handling has added enough appearance of age to confuse the furnishing collector of today, for a most important guide to the recognition of a fake is the evidence of use. For many years now the production of this type of fake has been low, the cost of skilled labour and the scarcity of the correct materials making it financially unworthwhile. Unfortunately the same cannot be said for the next category, the basically old but improved piece. This describes an article which, while remaining structurally unaltered, has the addition of decoration which would have been applied to only its finest contemporary counterpart. In general terms it describes a plain article converted by decoration into what appears to be a fine article. This was done mostly on eighteenth century mahogany furniture, but there are instances of this type of improvement occurring on country-made walnut furniture of the early eighteenth century.

The next hazard to confront the present day collector is easy to discern, but it leads directly to the type of copy most encountered today: the reproduction. The commercial mass-produced reproduction is made as near as possible to the designs of the antique, being slightly modified for use in the modern home and made with the latest and most up-to-date machinery. This type has been made since the turn of the century, but its very design and proportion are enough to give it away at first or, at most, second glance. The commercial reproduction was never intended to deceive, but to fulfil a demand for a style or fashion for the antique while remaining available in cost equivalent to any modern furniture of the time. However, vast quantities of extremely fine quality reproduction furniture have been and are being produced. These pieces are exact replicas of an original, with the minimum use of machinery in the production. Considerable time and skill is employed in research for authenticity of design and the achievement of a suitable patina, but the use of new timber and the absence of any signs of age underneath the article are sufficient for immediate recognition.

The article which has been altered structurally exists, like the recarved or improved piece, for one of two reasons. Furniture was altered during the nineteenth century because its original function was inadequate or because it was the wrong size for a certain position in the house. Bureau cabinets and bookcases were separated, sideboards reduced in width or length, clothes presses were made into wardrobes by removing the shelves. During the twentieth century, such alterations continued, but more often to increase falsely the value as refurnishing with antiques became more popular.

Having established the types of fakes most likely to be encountered the next step is to realise the various ways they can be identified. Unfortunately most of the unhelpful remarks inferring that years of study and practical experience are the only ways to learn are for the most part true. However, there are several guides rather than rules which may help to establish whether or not an article needs further examination. The most important single aspect in learning about old furniture is the ability to recognise that something is wrong. Knowing exactly what or where will come with time and experience, and when faced with such a problem piece there should be no hesitation in seeking further authoritative advice. It is equally important to avoid being too hasty in condemning outright an article where some doubt exists. The reason may be no more than an honestly but poorly executed repair. Providing this is not excessive and does not alter the character or use of the article it may be acceptable.

When viewing furniture formulate and memorise knowledge into brackets or headings which can be brought to mind quickly and easily. For example:

Date plus Shape plus Use plus Material.
Colour and surface condition (patina). Signs of wear.
Construction. Wood behaviour. Unexposed wood condition.

The first four should be compatible and contemporary and will signify the earliest date an article could have been made, i.e. Rococo style after 1730, tripod tea tables after 1720, mahogany after 1725. Having established that date, shape, use and material are contemporary, look for colour and surface condition.

Patina

Since craftsmen first took pride in their work, the outer surfaces of furniture have had some sort of preservative treatment when new. Following the decline in popularity during the sixteenth century of painting furniture after the application of a grain filler, the use of either an oil polish or a polish of beeswax and turpentine became standard practice. The main difference in the effect of these polishes is that through oxidisation the oil polish darkened the wood, whereas the beeswax sealed it and retained the mellow colour. The use of oil or wax polish continued on country furniture until the nineteenth century, but during the early Restoration period the use of varnish became most popular on all fine furniture. The first type of varnish used on most fine and particularly veneered furniture since the latter part of the sixteenth century was an oil and resin varnish. Thin coats of this mixture were applied to the surface of the wood, allowing time between each for the resin to dry out the oil. The surface was then rubbed with any one of a variety of mild abrasives which eventually filled the grain and left the timber well preserved, of good colour and ready for the first beeswaxing. Oil varnish was superseded during the 1670s by a spirit varnish. This consisted of spirits of wine and gum lac and was known as China varnish, introduced to England from the East where it had been used to preserve the fine lacquer work being imported into England at that time. As with the lacquer work itself, the materials were not available in western Europe to make China varnish, but before long we had discovered a suitable alternative. This was basically the same formula with a spirit base but either seed-lac or shell-lac was used instead of gum lac. The method of application was essentially the same as for the oil varnish. During the early 1820s an easier and inferior method of obtaining an immediate lustrous surface superseded the arduous task of varnishing. This was a formula introduced from France called 'french polishing' and consisted of soaking with shellac and spirit a wad or 'fad' of fine linen over padding. Several applications of this are made to the surface of the furniture until a glass-like finish is achieved. French polish is not as durable as oil varnish; it chips and wears away and is easily marked by heat or damp.

Unfortunately many pieces of earlier furniture have had the original patina stripped away to be french polished during the nineteenth and twentieth centuries. This detracts considerably from the merit of an article and can often be recognised by close examination of the grain.

To prepare a recently stripped and therefore open grained surface for french polishing the grain has first to be filled. During the nineteenth and early twentieth centuries ground pea-flower, whiting or plaster of Paris were most often used. These were stained a suitable colour and when dry the french polish was applied. Over the years the stain has bleached, leaving the grain marked with pale brown or white flecks. This does not occur on the surface of English furniture made before the early nineteenth century which retains its original finish or patina.

Whatever the colour of an article, it should have good patination. This describes the condition of the surface after years of waxing, the accumulation of grease and dirt and the multitude of small scratches resulting from general but not careless use.

During the eighteenth century both waxing and varnishing were used for polishing English furniture. Waxing was considered most suitable for chairs and smaller articles constructed in solid undecorated mahogany, and varnishing most suitable for most veneered surfaces.

Over a long period of time dirt and wax have not only filled the grain but have built up into small ridges above the surface. These can be seen when viewed obliquely against the light and cannot be reproduced, thus providing a guarantee of at least an old top, leg, rail or stretcher. On veneered surfaces, the varnish filled and sealed the grain, so there is no raised grain effect. Occasionally, fine ridges caused by the glue pushing through between the lines of stringing and crossbanding can be perceived with the fingertips, but by no means so noticeably as on the walnut veneered furniture of the late seventeenth century, see page 31. So for the most part it is the colour, absence of pale grain filler and the other elements of patina mentioned above which are the guides to the authenticity of surface condition on furniture of the late eighteenth century.

Signs of wear

Whereas the signs of use in the patina concern the outer surfaces, signs of wear relate to the effects of handling and the movements of working parts. Most early oak and walnut furniture originally stood on a stone floor that was frequently washed with water. Water will gradually rot wood and so one would expect to see signs of the feet having been eaten away and discoloration three to four inches up each leg. However, when the feet became unsteady it was common practice to cut them off as far as necessary and some early stools and chairs have the bottom rails at floor level due to this. Unfortunately a great many more have had the feet replaced and often so badly that true restoration is difficult. In order to examine the feet of a piece of furniture it has to be lifted up or tilted. When doing this note where the hands automatically take hold and where the ends of the fingers touch. It will be moved in the same way it has been moved since it was made and the hands and fingers will reach the same area. Such places should be darker than the rest of the underside. The natural oils of hands and fingers and the gradual accumulation of dust and dirt will have given the appearance of almost a patina. The rest of the underside should be dry looking, paler and perhaps dusty but not stained or polished. This applies without exception to chair and stool rails, drawer linings and table frames. Close scrutiny of the movement of working parts where two wood surfaces rub one against another should always reveal corresponding friction marks. The underneath of gate-leg table leaves where the leg pulls out in an arc to support the leaf, drawers and their runners and hinged doors that have fractionally dropped and rub on the frame or rail are typical instances.

While the faker seems to have ignored the simulation of hand holds underneath furniture, he has certainly spared no effort and imagination in achieving an instant patina on the outer surfaces or show wood. The effects of discoloration of most timbers can be gained by using chemicals. For the country faker in the past the most popular and efficient method of achieving age and in particular the rotted away feet and water-mark appearance was to stand the furniture in a regularly used stable. The acidity therein speeded the work of two hundred years into a matter of a few months. All manner of implements such as chains, small pieces of clinker as well as the conventional tools of the workshop were used to obtain the bruises and scratches that occur with constant use and form an integral part of the patina. But here, too, the enthusiastic faker so often gives himself away by overdoing the 'distressing'. This occurs when signs of use appear on places where it would not be expected and closer inspection reveals the distressing to be too regular in pattern.

Wood behaviour

As explained on page 10 the willow pegs should remain protruding from the inside top rails of English seventeenth century seat furniture, while their outside ends should be almost level with the surface of the leg or top. Not quite level, for timber contracts across the grain not along it. Therefore the peg might be fractionally smaller in diameter but it will be no shorter. The leg will have reduced in the same way, leaving the willow peg protruding just above the surface. This contraction applies to a greater or lesser degree to all timber and can be a useful guide, particularly when viewing country or very early furniture when often less well seasoned and matured woods were used. This is especially true and evident on farm house type oak tables with clamped ends. It is always good to see the clamps or cross members a little longer than the width of the top, see fig. 84, for the top will have shrunk across and so fractionally will the clamps but their lengths will have remained the same.

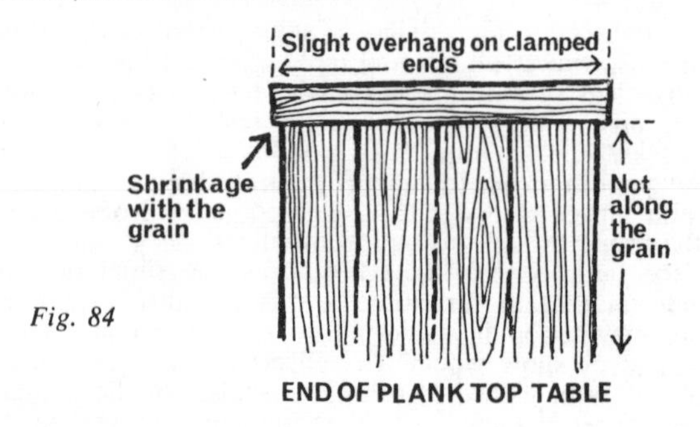

Fig. 84

Decoration

The fact that the decoration of an article is contemporary in design is insufficient evidence of its authenticity. For example, the carved shell found on rail or knee of most good quality Queen Anne furniture was a natural motif for the carver to reproduce on an originally plain article. When an eighteenth century chairmaker planned to decorate his chair with carving he allowed sufficient timber for the motif to stand proud of the outline of the leg or rail, see fig. 85. The recarver or faker had no such opportunity, and had therefore to cut into the timber to give the impression of relief. If the carving does not appear raised above the outline of a curved surface it is unlikely to be contemporary. For many years antique walnut furniture has commanded a higher price than oak, and many early oak bureaux and chests have been decorated with walnut veneer for that reason. However, with the exception of clock cases and pieces of the finest quality, English furniture of the seventeenth and early eighteenth century walnut period was rarely made with walnut veneered on to oak. Any oak visible, such as drawer linings and legs, should be solid and not veneered. Pine and deal were used for the carcases and drawer backs of veneered furniture and any piece found contrary to this is usually not English or of a later date. The veneer should be thick, being saw cut, see page 32, for it was not until the nineteenth century that thin knife cut veneer was produced.

During the last hundred years many two part pieces of furniture such as tallboys, bureau bookcases and cabinets have been separated; and many originally single pieces have had upper parts added. This was often done without thought or care for the original, thus providing several points to look for. Such two-piece furniture evolved from the cabinet or chest on stand of the late seventeenth century and the method of securing the

Fig. 85: A curved leg of the walnut or early mahogany period showing the carving on the knee standing proud of the outline of the curve, and the bold well formed claw and ball foot. When an article has been recarved at a later date the carving has to be below the surface of the curve.

top to the bottom remained unchanged. The stand had a retaining moulding on each side and the front to contain the base of the cabinet, see fig. 87. The moulding was seldom applied to the cabinet, and the top of the base which was to receive the cabinet was rarely veneered. When a chest of drawers was made as a dressing chest the top was intended to be used and visible and therefore decorated with veneer. When the same structure was made as the upper part of a tallboy the top was too high to be seen and therefore not veneered. Many top parts of tallboys have had feet added to make them into fashionable small chests, but the proportions of the large overhanging moulding at the top edge, and the similar moulding at the base which has to be made to balance, should be enough to arouse suspicion even if the top has been veneered at the time of its alteration.

Early eighteenth century handles or pulls were of the pendant, back plate and split pin type. These needed only a small hole in the centre of the drawer to take the tag and might have a small dent or pin hole ¾in. above and below the hole inside the drawer where the tag was fastened, see fig. 86. During the nineteenth century it was fashionable to remove any old metal handles and replace them with turned wood knobs. This type of handle originated during the last part of the eighteenth century but of much finer proportions than the bulbous creations applied ninety years later. The Victorian wood knob required a large hole, up to ½in. diameter, which can be seen inside the drawer, and was sometimes fixed by a screw thread worked into the drawer and turned on to the shank of the knob. To replace handles of the correct style this large hole has first to be plugged, an operation which is impossible to disguise. Nor should there be need to try. Modern castings of old handles have made it possible to restore the correct appearance to a

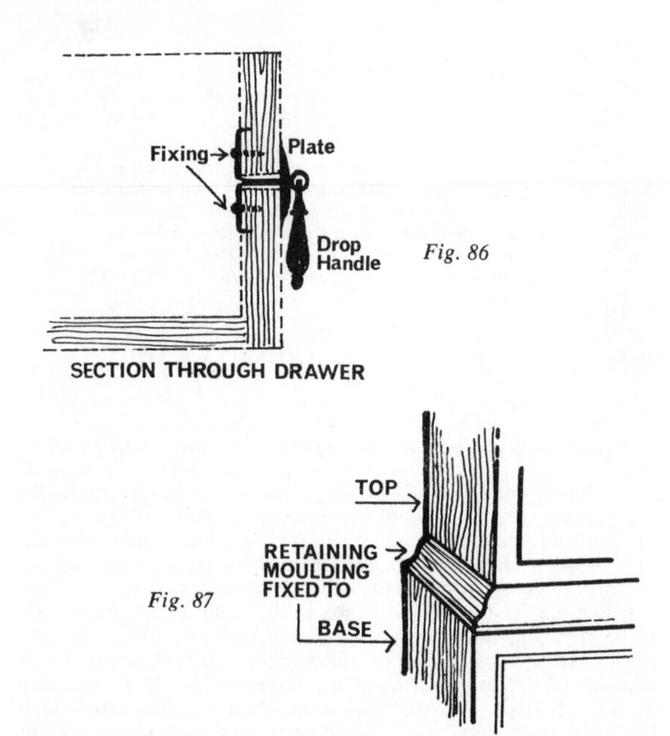

Fig. 86

Fig. 87

piece of furniture previously mutilated in this way, and the right style of handle can be gleaned from illustrations in eighteenth-century design books. A wrong handle immediately makes a piece of furniture look unbalanced and of bad proportions, therefore a new handle of original shape and style can be considered preferable to a Victorian or later one of the wrong size and pattern.

Woodworm

The evidence of woodworm is not necessarily a sign of age in furniture. The woodworm belongs to the same species as the death watch beetle and generally attacks furniture in poorly ventilated conditions. Woodworms eat into timber leaving small round holes visible on the surface. They then change direction and rest just below the surface where they go through various phases of development before emerging. Eggs are laid in the spring and the greatest activity is during the summer months. Use of a well known worm killer is the best treatment, but for severe damage an expert should be consulted. Woodworms burrow in and out of timber, never along the surface, so when any part of a piece of furniture has the surface disfigured with semi-circular channels and worm holes it must have been cut from timber previously used on another piece of furniture. No cabinet maker would have used ugly timber originally, but in an attempt to give 'age' to a piece the faker might.

Veneers

During the late seventeenth and early eighteenth centuries oak was seldom used as background material for walnut veneer, but during the middle of the eighteenth century it was much used in this way for mahogany veneer on better quality furniture. By the end of the eighteenth century mahogany itself was employed as background for veneers of satin wood, rosewood, kingwood, etc., and cedar was often used for the linings of small drawers in the finest quality pieces. The changes in the use of timbers form a pattern. Soft native timbers like deal were cheaper than oak yet adequate to be covered with walnut veneer and so were used in preference to oak. Mahogany, like walnut, was first used in the solid, but by the middle of the eighteenth century demand for fashionable furniture was so great that it was also used as veneer—on oak, for oak was used as background for the best French veneers, and our native soft woods had a tendency to warp. Solid oak had not been used for fashionable furniture for more than seventy years and, being less in demand, was now cheaper. By the end of the century mahogany was plentiful, less expensive, and could be cut to an even greater degree of fineness than oak, and was therefore considered suitable as both background and surface timber for the delicate furniture of that period.

The thickness of the veneer can also be a guide as to whether or not an article has been improved at a later date. Eighteenth century veneer was hand cut by saw, and was rarely less than one sixteenth of an inch thick. During the nineteenth century machine-cutting of veneer developed, and by 1900 paper thin veneers were being produced. An open or unfinished edge, a chipped corner, crack, or a piece of stringing which has come away are some of the places where the thickness of the veneer can be seen.

Just as the recarver improved originally plain eighteenth century furniture when the styles of Chippendale and Hepplewhite were so popular during the early 1900s, so the inlay worker applied his craft to similar pieces during the period of what is now known as Edwardian Sheraton. Whereas the absence of raised carved decoration is a guide to authenticity through the alteration of surface depth (see page 186), the re-inlayed piece provides a less obvious give-away. The wood removed to take decoration is replaced with panels of marquetry, stringing and crossbanding and its surface covered with layers of french polish. But where this has occurred the surface is slightly dented, and can be seen when viewed obliquely against the light. Oval shells, corner fans, box wood stringing and satinwood crossbanding are among the features most commonly employed by the re-inlayer, and it is basically through this man's lack of sense of proportion and ignorance of the eighteenth century original that it is possible to recognise his work. Inevitably it was the cheaper variety of article that underwent improvement and, as such, will always appear odd. Equally, it will have a highly polished surface, and the slightest sign of pale grain filler should lead to much closer examination of the inlay work. Inlay of the eighteenth century was applied to the better quality furniture and produced in the finest possible way. Only the contrasting grains of the different timbers reveal the joints between background and inlay, as if nothing but the thinnest razor blade had been used to cut the timber. There will be no space between the veneers except on previously uncared-for pieces when a minute ridge caused by glue coming through from the back might be just visible.

Alterations

One of the most popular articles to be improved by recarving has been the plain top, tripod base tea table (see page 80). The basic construction for both fine and plain tables of this type was the same. A square or rectangular platform, called a block, with two corners extended to form one inch long circular pegs, was fixed to the top of the column. The pegs fitted into holes in the runners which were then screwed to the underside of the top across the grain of the timber to prevent warping. The top was fastened in the horizontal position by a metal latch and plate. Thus the table could be tilted to stand against the wall when not in use. A variation is the bird-cage feature which enables the top to revolve as well as tip up, and which may be found on both fine and plain examples.

In order to establish whether the base and top are contemporary the top should be tilted and the areas where the block, underside of top and insides of runners have been in close contact should be carefully examined. As such tables were more often closed than tilted, these areas will have been less exposed to air and dust and should therefore appear slightly cleaner.

Friction marks on the insides of the runners and edges of the block caused when the table has been tilted should correspond. If the metal latch and ends of the tenons or bird-cage columns protrude slightly above the surface of the block, there should be corresponding bruises on the top made when it is closed. Such protrusions will have occurred because the block has shrunk slightly across the grain of the timber, see plate 66. The fact that timber shrinks across and not along the grain can be a useful guide on many occasions. For example, a tray top is 'dished' on a lathe and when new is perfectly circular; an original eighteenth century tray top rarely is, for the timber will have shrunk slightly; if a tray top is found to be exactly circular it is likely to have been altered recently, and further examination is advisable. An authentic tray top was turned from a thick piece of timber. A top intended to be plain was of thinner timber as there was no need to allow for dishing. Therefore when an originally plain top has been altered to a tray at a later date, the ends of the fixing screws for the runners will have been exposed. These can be easily cut off, but the holes will still be evident. To camouflage these the top will no doubt have been falsely scratched and bruised but their regularity should make them apparent. Note the position of the runners under the top and then carefully examine the top surface for two corresponding rows of eight equally spaced marks. The gallery edge supported on small turned pillars found on fine torcheres and tripod tables from the 1755-1775 period was invariably made in sections to give extra strength, whereas a 'pie-crust' or other raised and shaped edge was carved from the solid, which leads to another important guide regarding the authenticity of decoration. When an eighteenth century craftsman planned to have an article decorated with carving he allowed sufficient timber for the motif to stand proud of the basic outline of the curved leg or rail, see plates 27, 28, and 29. The recarver or faker had no such opportunity, and had therefore to cut into the already shaped surface to give the impression of relief. If the carving does not appear raised above the outline of a curved surface it is unlikely to be contemporary.

An example of a piece of furniture altered for utility reasons rather than an attempt to increase its value is the small work table illustrated in plate 69. Originally this had three shallow drawers below the fixed top to hold silks and cottons for needlework. A subsequent owner has had the upper two drawers removed, the top hinged, a new lock fitted using the existing keyhole in the top drawer, and the drawer fronts fixed to the carcase forming dummy drawers. Old lining paper is pasted roughly over the inside and marks caused when the securing blocks on the underside of the top were carelessly removed are clearly visible. As the hinges are apparently not the first it can be assumed that the alteration occurred some time ago. Similarly, for utility purposes, many articles of household furniture have been reduced in length, width and height; sideboards have had drawers removed to provide cupboard space, spinets have been converted to dressing tables, and many two-piece articles such as bureau-bookcases, cabinets and tallboys have been parted to make separate items of furniture. However, the poor proportions that inevitably result from such alterations are generally sufficient to create a doubt of authenticity. More recently a demand for taller case and cabinet furniture has caused originally single bureaux and secretaire chests to have upper cabinets added. Again proportion is an important aspect, but certain features in the original construction can be useful. The upper part should fit into a retaining moulding which was secured to the base, rarely to the upper part itself, and the top surface of a bureau or secretaire chest that was to be covered by a cabinet was rarely veneered.

The points discussed in this chapter are some of the faults likely to be encountered today on furniture of the 1720-1830 period. No one guide should be used alone but in conjunction with the text of the previous chapters and as many other aspects as possible. The inclusion or omission of one feature does not mean that an article is definitely genuine or fake: for instance, the lack of patina with the raised grain effect may have been caused by an enthusiastic polisher in the nineteenth century with no intent to deceive; alternatively its presence means only that the timber has always been the outer surface of something. A sense of proportion plays a large part in recognising that something is wrong, for however elaborate the decoration, furniture of the eighteenth century is always well balanced. It cannot be stressed too strongly that knowledge of the original is of paramount importance. Domestic English furniture was intended for use as well as decoration. Therefore it is only to be expected that working parts such as drawer runners, locks, hinges and woodjoints have become worn or damaged. Honest repair or replacement of such damage is quite acceptable providing it is well done, for furniture should, as far as possible, fulfil its original purpose. Treated with normal care and respect, old furniture can add warm atmosphere and character to a home, and most important of all, it will continue to improve in appearance while providing the owner with a pleasing and tangible piece of English history.

SOME TIMBERS USED DURING THE NINETEENTH CENTURY

For inexpensive and ordinary furniture; also country or provincial furniture:

ash; beech; birch; cedar; cherry; deal; pine; lime; fruit-woods; mahogany and walnut for veneer.

For best-quality furniture:

amboyna; coromandel; ebony; maple; oak; rosewood; satinwood; sandalwood; tulip-wood; walnut; zebra-wood.

For marquetry many woods were used. The following were found to take stain easily:

soft woods as above; holly; chestnut; pear; plum; sycamore.

The burr part of a tree was found to have decorative qualities when cut for veneer, two of the most popular being:

burr or 'bird's eye' maple; and burr oak.

Monarch	Date	Style	Materials
HENRY VIII	1509·1547	**TUDOR PERIOD** Gothic Ecclesiastical Renaissance Designs	**OAK** FRUIT WOODS · BEECH · ASH · ELM FOR COUNTRY FURNITURE LOW RELIEF CARVING · SOME PAINT (TEMPERA) & GUILDING
EDWARD VI	1547·1553		
MARY I	1553·1558		
ELIZABETH	1558·1603	**ELIZABETHAN PERIOD** Renaissance	INLAY USING FRUIT WOODS BEECH · ASH · HOLLY · SYCAMORE BONE · IVORY · MOTHER OF PEARL
JAMES I	1603·1625	**STUART PERIOD** Jacobean Renaissance Classicism Dutch Influence	
CHARLES I	1625·1649		TAPESTRY MANUFACTUREY AT MORTLAKE ESTBD 1620
COMMONWEALTH	1649·1660	Puritan Style	
RESTORATION	1660	**CAROLEAN PERIOD** Restoration Period 1st Chinoiserie Spanish Influence Netherlands	**WALNUT** CANE FOR SEATS & BACKS OF CHAIRS · VENEER PARQUETRY · OYSTERWOOD · LABURNUM · BOX HOLLY · FLORAL MARQUETRY USING HOLLY · FRUIT WOODS BURR WALNUT · EBONY ETC
CHARLES II	1649·1685		
JAMES II	1685·1689	Huguenot Influence	CARVED LIME & PINE FOR GESSO & GILDING · SILVERING ORIENTAL ENGLISH LACQUER
WILLIAM III MARY	1689·1702	Dutch Influence	ARABESQUE "SEAWEED" MARQUETRY USING BOX OR HOLLY & WALNUT
ANNE	1702·1714	Baroque	SOLID WALNUT
GEORGE I	1714·1727	**GEORGIAN PERIOD** Palladian Revival Baroque Roccoco Gothic 2nd Chinoiserie	**MAHOGANY** JAMAICAN · CUBAN
GEORGE II	1727·1760		
GEORGE III	1760·1820	**CLASSICAL REVIVAL** French Taste **REGENCY PERIOD** Græco Roman Neo·Classical Empire · Trafalgar 3rd Chinoiserie Egyptian Old French · Gothic Early English Revival	HONDURAS PAINTED FURNITURE SATINWOOD · KINGWOOD ETC EXOTIC WOODS FOR VENEERS MARQUETRY REVIVAL
REGENCY	1811·1820		
GEORGE IV	1820·1830		GILDING · LACQUER & BUHL
WILLIAM IV	1830·1837		
VICTORIA	1837·1901	**VICTORIAN PERIOD** Gothic (Mediæval) · Rustic Modern English · Art Nouveau Japanese	VARIOUS MATERIALS PAPIER MACHE
EDWARD VII	1901·1910	**EDWARDIAN PERIOD** Queen Anne, Sheraton Chippendale Style Reproductions	

Principal Designers	Principal Makers
INIGO JONES 1573·1651 THE ENGLISH PALLADIO' ONE TIME SURVEYOR GENERAL OF ROYAL BUILDINGS TO JAMES I & CHARLES I	**GERREIT JENSEN Circa 1680·1715** CABINET MAKER TO THE ROYAL HOUSEHOLDS OF CHARLES II & QUEEN ANNE
FRANCIS CLEYN DESIGNER AT MORTLAKE 1623·1658	**JOHN GUMLEY 1694·1729**
DANIEL MAROT Circa 1662·1752	**JAMES MOORE 1708·1726**
Wm KENT 1686·1748 (Palladian)	**ANDRÉ CHARLES BOULE 1642·1732**
Thos CHIPPENDALE 1718·1779 1ST EDITION OF HIS GENTLEMANS & CABINET MAKERS DIRECTOR PUBLISHED 1754 2ND 1755 3RD 1763	**Thos CHIPPENDALE 1718·1779**
Robt ADAM 1728·1792 CLASSICAL INFLUENCE FOLLOWING HIS RETURN TO ENGLAND IN 1758	**Thos CHIPPENDALE Jnr 1749·1822** IN PARTNERSHIP WITH THOMAS HAIG 1771·1796
BATTY & THOS LANGLEY PUBLISHED IN 1740 · CITY & COUNTRY BUILDER'S & WORKMAN'S TREASURY OF DESIGNS · FRENCH STYLE & GOTHIC	**MATHIAS LOCK 1740·1769** VARIOUS PUBLICATIONS CIRCA 1740·1769 CARVER AS WELL
Geo HEPPLEWHITE ·· 1786 1ST EDITION OF HIS 'THE CABINET MAKERS & UPHOLSTERERS GUIDE PUBLISHED 1788, 2ND 1789, 3RD 1794	**W.&J.HALFPENNY Circa 1750** ARCHITECTS & DESIGNERS OF FURNITURE GOTHIC & CHINESE FATHER & SON WORKING TOGETHER
Thos SHERATON 1751·1806 1ST EDITION OF HIS THE CABINET MAKERS & UPHOLSTERERS DRAWING BOOK PUBLISHED 1791·1794	**Geo HEPPLEWHITE ·· 1786**
INCE & MAYHEW 1758·1810 1759-63 PUBLISHED 'UNIVERSAL SYSTEM OF HOUSEHOLD FURNITURE	**Wm HALLETT 1707·1781** MOST POPULAR CABINET MAKER DURING REIGN OF GEORGE II
HENRY HOLLAND 1746·1806 ARCHITECT · STRICT GRAECO-ROMAN STYLE.	**Wm & John LINNELL Circa 1720·1763**
Thos HOPE 1769·1831 PUBLISHED HOUSEHOLD FURNITURE & INTERIOR DECORATION 1807	**Geo SEDDON 1727·1801**
Geo SMITH Circa 1780·1840 PUBLISHED 'A COLLECTION OF DESIGNS FOR HOUSEHOLD FURNITURE & AND INTERIOR DECORATION 1808	**Wm VILE & JOHN COBB Circa 1750·1765** A MOST FAMOUS MANUFACTURING PARTNERSHIP
LE GAIGNEUR Circa 1815	**Wm INCE & JOHN MAYHEW Circa 1758·1810**
AUGUSTUS WELBY PUGIN 1812·1852 GOTHIC DECORATION ON HOUSES OF PARLIAMENT	**Robt & Thos GILLOW Circa 1740-1811** MAKERS OF FURNITURE LANCASTER & LATER (CIRCA 1760) LONDON
T.KING PRODUCED 'THE MODERN STYLE OF CABINET WORK 1839 LIKENED TO DESIGNS BY GEORGE SMITH AND THE LATER EGYPTIAN' TASTE & CABINET WORK SUPPLEMENT	**MARSH & TATHAM 1795**
H.W. & A.ARROWSMITH 'HOUSE DECORATOR & PAINTERS GUIDE ALL STYLES 1840	**LE GAIGNEUR Circa 1815** BUHL WORK (BOULE)
HENRY WHITTAKER Circa 1847 DESIGNER	**Geo BULLOCK Circa 1817**
Chas EASTLAKE 1836·1906 HINTS ON HOUSEHOLD TASTE	**T.B.JORDAN** WOODCARVING MACHINE 1845
BRUCE TALBERT DESIGNER · APPEARANCE OF MEDIAEVAL 'WOODWORK PEGGED JOINTS ETC	**MORRIS, MARSHALL & FAULKNER & CO 1861**
RICHARD CHARLES DESIGNER	**WARWICK SCHOOL OF CARVING** CIRCA 1850 (STARTED)
E.W.GODWIN DESIGNER	**GREAT EXHIBITION 1851**
CHRISTOPHER DRESSER JAPANESE TASTE	**HOLLAND & SONS** 23 MOUNT STREET · LONDON · EXHIBITED AT **INTERNATIONAL EXHIBITIONS** PARIS 1855.1867 · LONDON 1862 · 1871
	J.G.GRACE & SONS 1745·1899 FAMILY FIRM

<table>
<tr><th>MONARCH</th><th>DATE</th><th>IMPORTANT STYLES IN ORDER OF INTRODUCTION</th><th>MATERIALS</th></tr>
<tr><td>WILLIAM IV</td><td>1830-1837</td><td>Late Classical-
Egyptian
Etruscan
Heavy formal-foliate carving in low relief
Old French-
Influence of early & mid 18thC French</td><td>Highly figured mahogany veneers
Rosewood
Gilding and ormolu mounts
Papier-mâché
Carton pierre</td></tr>
<tr><td>VICTORIA</td><td>1837-1901</td><td>Mid 1840s Gothic Revival
Accent on ecclesiastical architecture of the Perpendicular, Early English and Decorated periods
Medieval
romantic historical influences of the Tudor and Elizabethan periods
Italian and English
Renaissance Revival
Late 17thC bobbin and barley-sugar twist turning
Rustic. Secular Gothic
All above evident at the 1851 Exhibition
Warwick School
oak carving of Grinling Gibbons influence
Arts & Crafts Movement-
Glueless construction, less surface decoration, sombre colours. Pegged joints
Japanese Influence
Art Nouveau
Revivals of Queen Anne
Chippendale styles
Adam & Sheraton</td><td>Oak
Cast iron & steel sprung seats
Walnut
Deep buttoned upholstery
Heavy drapes
Berlin needlework
Walnut, solid and veneer
Porcelain inset panels
Marquetry
Maple
Satinwood
Ebony
Gilt metal
Black and tortoiseshell inlay
Buhl & 'contre' buhl
Painted 'whitewood'
Bentwood bamboo & Cane
Lacquer panels
Very thin machine cut veneers of:- walnut/mahogany
Inlaid & painted satinwood, ivory, ebony
Metal panels</td></tr>
<tr><td>EDWARD VII</td><td>1901-1910</td><td>Functional & utility designs:
Early Art Deco</td><td>Pine, deal, beech, birch.</td></tr>
</table>

IMPORTANT EVENTS	SOME PRINCIPAL DESIGNERS·MAKERS·FACTORS AND PERIODICALS
International Exhibitions *	AUGUSTUS WELBY PUGIN DESIGNS FOR NEW HOUSES OF PARLIAMENT ECCLESIASTICAL GOTHIC (SIR CHARLES BARRY·ARCHITECT)
	SIR G. STREET THE NEW LAW COURTS
	E.BURNE-JONES, W.BURGES, C.L.EASTLAKE
	R.BRIDGENS, R.BITMEAD, C.DRESSER
	A.H.MACKMURDO, B.TALBERT, H.WHITTAKER
	C.VOYSEY, P.WEBB, SIR MATTHEW DIGBY WYATT
T.B.JORDAN Woodcarving machine 1845	J.CRACE & SONS 1745-1899 HOLLAND & SONS, MOUNT ST, LONDON H.W.& A.ARROWSMITH
GREAT EXHIBITION* 1851 London	C.R.ASHBEE
New Houses of Parliament formally open 1852	JOHN C.LOUDON 1783-1843 ENCYCLOPAEDIA OF COTTAGE, FARM & VILLA ARCHITECTURE (ISSUES FROM 1833-1867)
PARIS EXHIBITION* 1855	MESSRS JACKSON & GRAHAM, LONDON GILLOW OF LONDON
Japanese Show at GREAT EXHIBITION* London 1862	JENNENS & BETTRIDGE (PAPIER-MÂCHÉ) J.M.WILLCOX, T.H.KENDALL COOKES (WARWICK SCHOOL)
Pre-Raphaelite Society formed by Rossetti London 1843	A.STONE & SON (HIGH WYCOMBE & LONDON) WILLIAM MORRIS 1834-96 ESTABLISHED MORRIS, MARSHALL, FAULKNER IN 1861 AND THE KELMSCOTT PRESS IN 1891
PARIS 1867*	JOHN BLY Established 1891
VIENNA 1873*	S.BLAKE (MARQUETRY)
PHILADELPHIA 1876*	MONBRO (OLD FRENCH)
PARIS 1878*	H.ROGERS (BOXWOOD CARVINGS)
Art Workers Guild formed 1883	WRIGHT & MANSFIELD (ADAM STYLE) BLYTH & SON
LONDON 1886*	EDWARDS & ROBERTS
Arts & Crafts Exhibition Socy formed 1888	LASENBY LIBERTY SIR AMBROSE HEAL
Shows 1889 " 90 " 93 " 96 " 99	1849 Art Journal
PARIS 1889*	1860 Cabinet Makers Monthly Journal of Design
CHICAGO 1893*	1877 The Cabinet Makers Pattern Book
PARIS 1900*	1873 The Furniture Gazette 1880 Decoration
GLASGOW 1901*	1893 Studio 1901 Connoisseur
BRUSSELS 1910*	1902 The Art Workers Quarterly

Fig. 88: The pedestal block of the table illustrated in plate 93, showing the brass plate engraved and enamelled with the Design Registration Mark for 14th December 1847. These marks are found on nineteenth-century English ceramics, metalwork, furniture, etc., and from 1842 can be read in the following way:

The figure at the top of the diamond denotes the class of material, in this case furniture.

The letter at the top inside the diamond denotes the year.

The left hand letter denotes the month.

The right hand number denotes the day of the month.

The number at the bottom is the parcel number.

In 1868 the inside letters and numbers were moved one space in a clockwise direction, there remaining until 1883. Thus:

The day of the month was at the top. The year was on the right. The month was at the bottom. The parcel number was on the left.

When the letter for the year is at the top, date can be ascertained from the following table;

1842 = X	1848 = U	1854 = J	1860 = Z	1866 = Q
1843 = H	1849 = S	1855 = E	1861 = R	1867 = T
1844 = C	1850 = V	1856 = L	1862 = O	
1845 = A	1851 = P	1857 = K	1863 = G	
1846 = I	1852 = D	1858 = B	1864 = N	
1847 = F	1853 = Y	1859 = M	1865 = W	

When the letter for the year is at the right, date can be ascertained from the following table;

1868 = X	1873 = F	1878 = D	
1869 = H	1874 = U	(except 1st to 6th March 1878 = W)	
1870 = C	1875 = S	1879 = Y	
1871 = A	1876 = V	1880 = J	1882 = L
1872 = I	1877 = P	1881 = E	1883 = K

The months and corresponding letters are as follows:

January = C or O, February = G, March = W, April = H, May = E, June = M, July = I, August = R, September = D, October = B, November = K, December = A.

Exceptions: December 1860 = K, September 1st-19th 1857 = R.

INDEX

INDEX

Printed by C. I. Thomas & Sons (Haverfordwest) Ltd.,
Press Buildings, Merlins Bridge, Haverfordwest, Pembs.